PRAISE FOR *Principled Leader*

Infused with a deep appreciation for the human experience, this inspiring book is packed with strategies to joyfully live in service of others. Putting these principles into practice will cultivate positive learning communities built on empathy, respect, trust, and gratitude. If you want to grow as a leader and nurture healthy relationships, this book is for you!

Lainie Rowell
Experienced Educator and District Leader
International Consultant, Author of
Evolving with Gratitude and *Evolving Learner*

Bobby Pollicino has created a comprehensive compendium of sound advice for helping anyone become a better leader—but not just that. This book is full of advice that will help you be a better individual, capable of achieving your purpose and investing in your passions, as well as helping those you lead achieve their goals.

Michael B. Horn
Author of *From Reopen to Reinvent*

In *Principled Leader*, Bobby shares the ideas that have been the core of his growth as a leader. Having worked with Bobby for over a decade, I've had the opportunity to witness his evolution. An avid reader, Bobby weaves in stories from books that have inspired his personal practice and explains how he has applied these lessons to a school setting. Bobby is disciplined in his approach and continually reflects on his practice. It is wonderful to see him share forward what he has learned as a teacher, coach, division head, and father to guide others.

Stacey Roshan
Educator, Author, Speaker, Consultant

Whether you are in the field of education or not, I highly recommend this book. From leadership, relationships, reflection, standards and goals, this book is something I wish I had read in my early twenties. It is rare that you find a book that has simple to understand strategies and actionable steps you can immediately implement. If you are looking to become a better version of yourself - pick up *Principled Leader*, you will be glad you did!

Christopher J. Wirth, MPM
Author, Speaker, Coach & Podcast Host,
Founder of No Quit Living and The Positivity Tribe

As I read *Principled Leader,* I reflected on the practices I've used and developed over the past 30 years in education. This book allowed me "the opportunity to learn and grow in my experiences." *Principled Leader* is not only an engaging and quick read but has actual strategies, which can be used daily. Bobby spotlights campus meetings, timely communication, climate & culture, self-care, setting core values, being true to your vision, etc. Any reader can use this book as a beginning guide, a 101 to educational leadership. Finally, I'm a quote guy, and he masterfully embeds famous quotes to daily events that take place on a campus. If you are looking to sharpen your skills and become a better version of yourself, this book is the right tool.

Josh Tovar
Principal

Bobby Pollicino has crushed it with *Principled Leader*. It has helped me, and it will do the same for any present or future leader. Easy to read, understand and implement. *Principled Leader* will make you and your organization better. Period!

Eric Kapitulik
Founder and CEO, The Program Leadership

Bobby Pollicino shows what it means to practice what you preach. This book is built on the foundation of principles because they are the building blocks of successful leadership. Each chapter includes actionable steps that you can begin the moment you put down the book. In order to be a Principled Leader, you must develop goals based on who you are and who you want to be. Readers, Bobby shows you exactly how to turn the life that you are living into a life of purpose and direction. Get ready to launch yourself into the next level!

Brandon Beck
Teacher, Speaker, Coach, Podcast Host

Wow - Mr. Pollicino's first book is a MUST READ!! Changing the culture of education is a daunting but important task. That is why *Principled Leader* should be required reading for anyone who considers themselves an educational leader. Bobby's fresh approach to leadership serves as a practical and impactful guide for changing the culture in our profession!

Jared Smith
School Superintendent, Bestselling Author

Bobby Pollicino has crafted a sincere tome on leadership. With his invitational tone, *Principled Leader* will prove to be a go-to book for repeated references for both current and aspiring leaders. I am fortunate to know Bobby, and this book is a beautiful reflection of a true leader. Read, savor, and share Bobby's words. There aren't many leadership books out there reaching for the empathetic level that Bobby so successfully hits in this book. I needed this book 20 years ago when I started my leadership journey. Today, I am grateful that this book is in my life. Every leader needs a reboot for their core and Bobby Pollicino has provided a sustainable resource in the pages you are about to visit again and again.

Sean Gaillard
Principal, Author, Podcaster

BOBBY POLLICINO
PRINCIPLED LEADER

Principled Leader

Copyright © by Bobby Pollicino
First Edition 2022

All rights reserved.

No part of this publication may be reproduced in any form, or by any means, electronic or mechanical, including photocopying, recording, or any information browsing, storage or retrieval system, without permission in writing from the publisher.

Cover Photo by Geran de Klerk on Unsplash

Road to Awesome, LLC.

To my amazing wife, Lauren,
for her unyielding love and support.

I am a better person today because of her and strive to be better each day forward because of her.

TABLE OF CONTENTS

Foreward………………………………………………1

Introduction……………………………………….…5

Chapter 1 – Life Principles……………………………13

Chapter 2 – Relationship Principles……………..…… 35

Chapter 3 – Leadership Principles…………..………. 63

Chapter 4 – Leadership Strategies…………………. 101

Chapter 5 – Fitness Principles………………………. 121

Chapter 6 – Decision Making……………………….139

Conclusion…………………………………………149

Glossary……………………………………………151

Suggested Reading to Further Your Growth………...155

Acknowledgements…………………………………157

About the Author……………………………………161

FOREWARD
by Christopher D. Connors

Transformational leadership is born from an earnest desire to learn, grow and get better for yourself everyday. To inspire transformation in others, we must start "local" and begin the hard work of leadership development with ourselves. You may be an administrator, school leader, teacher or at the start of your career journey. Wherever you find yourself, you're sure to keep growing each day if you dedicate yourself to a lifelong education in personal development and growth.

By starting to read *Principled Leader*, I believe you're well on your way to achieving a goal, strengthening a strength and discovering something new about yourself that will increase your emotional intelligence.

In my work with organizations and leaders, I talk often about the power of emotionally intelligent leadership.

You → Why → Others.

As a leader, to be at your best each day and help others, it's imperative to be self-aware, and clear in your goals, intentions and desired impact. You're best served to have clarity around your purpose (why you're doing what you're doing) and to establish your values to solidify the bedrock foundation of your leadership.

Following Bobby's journey over the past several years, and working with him throughout the course of a pivotal school year, I observed his leadership values and principles first hand. I know the words you're about to read in these pages come from direct application, lessons learned and experience. He is honest, sincere, straightforward, caring and both a dedicated student and advanced practitioner in the art of leadership.

I've found great leaders aren't fluffy. They provide vision. They're focused. Great leaders are self-motivated and they use their drive to help and empower the people around them. You can be a principled leader by being both empathetic, candid and direct. When you lead with values and principles, you'll earn the admiration and respect of others. You'll inspire belief in people's hearts and help them to build a growth mindset. That's what authentic connection and elevating others is all about.

The best leadership is by example. I've had the privilege of coaching and working with CEO's, leaders and executives across major industries. I'm always most impressed by the leaders who walk the walk. Legendary Tennessee women's basketball coach Pat Summitt once famously said, "I would not ask my staff or my team to do anything that I wouldn't do myself." Bobby is that principled leader who truly invests the time in his own growth and inspires the people he leads to invest in their own development.

What you'll find in these pages is a playbook for how to lead with confidence and courage, how to manage people, but best of all, how to be right for yourself first so you can be your best for others. Bobby shows you how to provide constructive feedback, while also recognizing the valuable contributions of your people. These are powerful leadership tools for engagement and retention.

Principled Leader is organized into concise, easy-to-read sections that help you understand through storytelling and time-tested leadership principles what it means to lead from the heart and act with integrity. By acquiring a leadership skill set that is built on a rock-solid foundation of honesty, trust and empathy, you will learn how to bring people along with you on your leadership journey.

Leadership isn't easy. As Tom Hanks said in *A League of Their Own*, "If it wasn't hard, everyone would do it. The hard is what makes it great."

The journey you're taking by aiming to improve and grow won't be easy, but it will be rewarding. By applying the principles herein with consistency and discipline, you'll take steps each day toward reaching your potential and impacting lives in a profound way.

Now is your opportunity to "do the work" and discover your own brand of leadership. The resources, tools and examples provided in this book will help elevate the way you see yourself, habits you set and the actions you take. Leadership is truly about influence—using your talents, passion, skills and experience to positively impact the people around you. It's not easy, but it's always worth it. The influence you can have on the people you lead can positively change their lives forever.

INTRODUCTION

"I made a prosperous voyage when I suffered a shipwreck."
- Zeno

Sitting in a weekly administrative team meeting, my head of school looked at me and asked if I had my finger on the pulse of the faculty. I replied matter-of-factly, "No." It was a simple statement, and it was true. I was in a role that I thought I was prepared for but, in that moment, it became clear that I was not. I said the right things at times but not all the time. More importantly, I was not leading in a sustainable manner. I knew what got me to the position as an independent school division head. I also realized that I knew what I needed to do to stay there and be effective. I am grateful for that question and the path it has led me to, which I continue on today.

Stepping back, it is clear to me that much of what got me to where I was and the struggle I was having as a leader stemmed from my experiences as a child, teenager, college student athlete and young professional. There were countless occasions along the way when I learned and saw examples of positive leadership as well as negative leadership. There were lessons learned that did not stick until later in life when I looked back on them.

I grew up in a middle class working family in upstate New York with my two parents and an older brother. Our father enlisted in the United States Marine Corps after graduating from high school during the height of the Vietnam War. After his tour in Vietnam, he returned to the States and embarked on a career of service for the United States Post Office, Veteran's Organizations, and as a volunteer firefighter. Many of the lessons learned were about hard work, commitment and loyalty. All of those were more important than how one felt in the moment. That brings me back to the question from my head of school. I was not focused on how the faculty felt, I was more focused on whether or not they did their job and were committed to the mission of the school. To be clear, I do not view this as a negative example of leadership, but rather a different style or approach, perhaps one that would be considered old school and not sustainable.

In high school, as the captain of our varsity boys' lacrosse team, I recall imploring our team to have greater commitment to the goals of repeating as sectional champs and returning to the state tournament as we did the year before. I would push in practice or in the locker room, but I also know that my actions outside of that time did not always match my words. I would ask for greater buy-in or support when it was convenient or seemed necessary but not when it mattered most, which was in the classroom, hallways, or on the weekends. I can still remember asking the team to take advantage of the opportunity afforded us instead of taking advantage of the situation, yet those words would ring hollow at times on a Saturday night. I thought I was being a good leader. In hindsight, I was not because I did not lead when it was difficult.

I was fortunate enough to play college lacrosse at Washington College, which has a historically strong program in the Centennial Conference in Division III. We had a tremendous three-year run from 1996 to 1998 that included three straight national championship appearances, one of which ended in victory. Heading into 1999, we had a new coach and a strong nucleus returning. The year did not go as I had hoped for a variety of reasons, including a broken wrist during a fall tournament at the Naval Academy. This put me behind in my training and ability to practice heading into spring of senior year. I worked to get back but was not getting the playing time I thought I deserved. I questioned the coaching decisions and my place on the team. It was not until midway through the season that I realized I needed to focus on what I could control - my effort and attitude. I began working out in the mornings, which was not something we did during the season. One morning, Coach saw me and said I was starting the next game. There is no fairy tale ending, with me going on to lead the team to ultimate victory and back to the national championship (we lost in the quarterfinals that year), but there was a lesson. If you focus on what you can control - your effort and attitude - there will be opportunities. This lesson did not stay with me nearly as well as I would have liked. I would often fall back into a more pessimistic mindset even as my career began in education.

One opportunity came not long after graduating when I was named head lacrosse coach at a small private school in Virginia. At 24 years old, I thought I knew all that I needed to be a successful coach. I took much of what I learned growing up into that role. Similar to the question asked 15 years later by my head of school, I did not know how my team was feeling or what they needed. I made decisions based on what I thought they needed. Again, I thought I was being a good leader, but looking back, I had much to learn about modeling for my team and coaches. I demanded excellence and commitment but did not seek feedback from other coaches or the players. I did not always explain why I was making certain choices or plans. It was more of an authoritative leadership style and certainly one that did not involve listening.

In moving to my next school, I had more opportunities to take on leadership roles and administrative positions. With this increased responsibility, I let other aspects of life slip away, such as mental and physical fitness. I did not take the time to read or exercise. I put the needs of students and players ahead of my own children and family at times. My work/home experience was not in harmony and was heavily tilted towards work. This mindset was fed by the increasing amount of responsibilities and duties I was offered administratively and in becoming a head coach again. The one area of clarity for me was in the role of head coach as I knew and understood my why, my purpose. I was there to provide an experience for my lacrosse players that would prepare them for playing in college and to overcome challenges they would face beyond the field. I was working to build young men of character. When I stepped away from that role and into a role as a division head, I lost my why and did not make a concerted effort to find it. I was reacting to the world around me instead of consciously responding.

I want to help individuals who currently find themselves in a similar situation or have aspirations for greater leadership opportunities. If we are not careful, we find ourselves drifting through life simply reacting to what happens to us. We have a conscious choice we can make every day about how to move forward. Each of our decisions provides us with another choice or option.

It is true that our lives do not get easier or simpler as we get older. The number of responsibilities increases and the time available to meet these responsibilities seems to decrease. Clearly, we have the same amount of time available (24 hours and 7 days) as we always did, but too often, we allow others to fill it and tell us how to use it. In some cases, this is our own doing. For example, when we opt into a relationship, we should give this person our time and attention. If we choose to have children, we are making the conscious decision to give our time and attention to another human. As we take on greater responsibility at our place of employment, we might find our use of time dictated by others. How you spend your time and who dictates your time is a direct reflection of the choices you are making. Each individual has to take ownership and invest time in a way that will help them live out their why.

We complicate our lives further by making choices that do not help to simplify our day-to-day experience. We spend time aimlessly searching the web, scrolling through social media, bingeing on Netflix, shopping on Amazon. We stay up late, drink too much alcohol or eat unhealthy foods. The list is different for each of us, but we end up in the same place: making choices that result in a lack of time in a complex world with limited control of what is happening to us.

The reality is that we do have time, and we can make choices to simplify our life. We have to identify our priorities and act on those each day. Even that last sentence is a bit complicated seeing as you can only have so many priorities that you focus on at one time. In Greg McKeown's book, *Essentialism: The Disciplined Pursuit of Less*, he shares that the word priority first appeared in the English language in the 1400s and existed in the singular form up until the 1900s when it was pluralized. We have to identify a few important priorities and focus only on them so we can give each their proper attention. This is much easier said than done. In order to help us get clarity or set parameters for ourselves, we need a set of principles to go along with our core values and priorities.

We are faced with challenges every day and we can either react or respond to them. Moving forward in this book, I will often refer to challenges as opportunities because that is one of the first steps: choosing to respond and not react. When we respond, we are in control of our emotions, and we are able to see the opportunity for what it truly is. According to Epictetus,

> The chief task in life is simply this: to identify and separate matters so that I can say clearly to myself which are externals not under my control, and which have to do with the choices I actually control. Where, then, do I look for good and evil? Not to uncontrollable externals but within myself to the choices that are my own…

The Stoics are a great place to look for ideas and suggestions to recenter yourself and gain clarity. Beyond looking at the work of others, we need to identify key principles in our own life by which we choose to abide. The ones I am sharing in this book are by no means exhaustive, but the list is too long to memorize. They serve as guides for you to reference when faced with various opportunities in your personal and professional life. You can look at the opportunities before you and find a principle or mental model in this book that will guide you on your path. With the volume of principles being what it is, you also need to consider your core values or tenets by which you choose to live. This list should be far shorter, and quite easy, for you to think about each day and in each experience. When developing your list of values, it is important to remember the teachings of Frederick the Great, "He who defends everything, defends nothing." With that said, keep your list between three and five values. I focus on three core values:

1. **INTEGRITY** - all decision-making is rooted in this core value. Can I look at myself in the mirror and feel good about the decisions I made today?
2. **DISCIPLINE** - the ability to focus on what needs to be done versus what I want to do. It drives me to get up at 4:30 a.m. every day to exercise.
   - "There are 2 pains in life: discipline and regret." - Bill Curry
   - "Very few go astray who comport themselves with restraint." - Confucius
   - "If a person puts even one measure of effort into following ritual and the standards of righteousness, he will get back twice as much." --Xunzi

3. **COURAGE** - we need to exhibit daily courage to see everyday challenges as opportunities and make decisions that may not be popular.

Each of these core values play out in various ways throughout the book and in my daily life. I hope that seeing them will help you develop your own values to use in your daily life. If you want to find success in your career and build healthy, lasting relationships in your life, consider how you can implement the principles in this book.

This book is written for current and aspiring leaders who are seeking tangible and practical ways to grow. It is intended to show you the lessons I have learned along the way and resources you can use as a leader. The past five years have been transformational for me, and I am grateful to share my journey with you.

CHAPTER 1
LIFE PRINCIPLES

We have a choice to either drift through life or be intentional in charting a path. It is important to note that we need to consistently evaluate our approach and decisions as it can be easy to fall back into old habits or patterns. When there are changes in our career or personal life, we may regress. If that happens, we need to evaluate and reflect on our why so we can be the best version of ourselves and serve others. We must know our why.

KNOWING YOUR WHY: It is important to live with purpose every day, otherwise we find ourselves drifting and simply reacting to what happens to us. While we cannot control all that happens in our lives, we can make decisions connected to our larger purpose. In Simon Sinek's famous Ted Talk, *Start with Why*, and in his book of the same name, he explains to the audience the importance of knowing your why and how it can guide you. It serves as your North Star and helps you remain focused on growing and improving every day. At the beginning of this book, I referenced a story from early on in my role as a division leader. Before I stepped into that role, I knew my why as a coach and dean of students. As a dean, I was working towards developing young men and women into people of character. In my role as a coach, I was preparing young men to be successful on and off the lacrosse field, including at the collegiate level if they desired. This was clear to me and drove my decisions and actions. I did not stop to truly look at how this would change with a new job, responsibilities, and expectations. Due to this, I was drifting and not finding success in my first year. I lost that clarity in my new role as a division director. The summer after my first year in the position, I read two pivotal texts that would help me start on a path to greater self-knowledge and success. The first book I read was *Start with Why: How Great Leaders Inspire Everyone to Take Action*. It helped me see the need to clarify this in my own mind and for the faculty. It also helped me solidify our work as a faculty as we discussed our why as a teaching community - both collectively and individually. This helped create a shared purpose, which is necessary in any successful organization. It was at this point that I developed my new why: develop leaders who will inspire and positively impact future leaders. The second book I read was *Warfighting* from the United States Marine Corps. While this may seem like an odd reading choice while working in schools, we should all take lessons from successful organizations that are perceived to be outside of our sphere of influence. This text helped sharpen my focus and understanding of leadership. Perhaps more importantly, it served as a reminder of the importance of living by a set of standards and principles of which you can be proud.

SET STANDARDS AND LIVE BY THEM: Once you have established your why you need standards to help you live your purpose. These standards ensure you are living your why daily.

UNDERSTAND THE DIFFERENCE BETWEEN STANDARDS AND GOALS: Setting goals is important as they help us strive to move forward in a positive manner. Standards are the behaviors that guide our decision-making and support our goals. We set goals in life to ensure we are not complacent, professionally or personally, and to strive for improvement.

We may not reach every fitness goal or get the promotion exactly when we want. That simply means we need to recalibrate, and go after it again. It is okay to fall short of a goal because it requires us to stretch and grow. If you regularly meet every goal, the bar may be too low, and you should reconsider how much you ask of yourself. That said, if you failed to meet the goal because you are not meeting your standards, a different approach is required. As a division head, I need to get out of my office and into classrooms. I need to set a standard for myself to be out of the office for a specific amount of time each day. I also may set a goal to visit three classrooms every day. If I do not meet the standard first, it is impossible for me to meet my goal. I have to leave my office (the standard) to get into a classroom for a visit (the goal). I might end up running into a colleague, teacher, or student on my walk that can keep me from getting into three classrooms for a visit. I might need to look at the goal and recalibrate the standard. If I set a goal to get healthy and part of that goal includes a standard of exercising daily, I need to meet the standard before I look at the outcomes of my goals. If I fail to meet the standard, the goal is no longer of value to me. If I am meeting the standard but did not reach the goal, then I need to look at other aspects of my health; perhaps my diet or alcohol consumption is holding me back.

RECOGNIZE WHEN YOU OR OTHERS CHOOSE TO RATIONALIZE CHANGES TO THE STANDARD: It is easy to make an excuse and rationalize a change to your standards.

There are times in a school year when we are busier than others. This can be at the end of a semester when we are reviewing report cards or teacher comments. If we go back to the standard of getting out of the office every day for a set amount of time, I can convince myself it is not possible because of the additional work. I tell myself I will get back to the standard next week after I take care of the more pressing work. I fell victim to the tyranny of the urgent. We need to detach and determine if this is really the case. Can I maintain my standard and meet the additional responsibilities? Perhaps I cannot do that, and if that is true, own it, accept it and move forward. We also face these questions and challenges in our personal life. For example, if you normally get up to exercise every morning but start taking holidays or weekends off, acknowledge it, own it and evaluate why you are making that decision. Maybe your body needs the rest due to the intensity of your workouts or you prefer to stay in bed with your partner or you want to be available to your children to make breakfast. Whatever the reason is you are making the choice, own it. If you make a conscious decision to not drink alcohol during the week and find yourself attending work happy hours on Thursday at your new job, acknowledge it, own it and evaluate the decision. Is it truly necessary to attend these happy hours or are you just convincing yourself it is? If you are not careful, the rationalization of standards will creep into all aspects of your life. As Clayton Christensen said, "It's easier to hold onto your principles 100% of the time than 98% of the time." Once you make that first excuse, it gets easier to make the next one.

BUILD AROUND GOALS – NOT TASKS: We set goals for various reasons. Some goals are tied to our personal life, others to our professional life. Sometimes, we set goals because someone else asks us to. Regardless of the goal, it should drive your day-to-day decision making instead of a task list. Too much of our life is task-driven. We make lists and cross things off our list to feel a sense of accomplishment. There are some goals that take months or years to accomplish, and if we do not have the immediate reward or feedback, it is hard to maintain the discipline. However, if you build your daily schedule around steps that help you reach your goal, you become more fulfilled, and you are more likely to reach that goal.

It is important for school administrators to focus on servant leadership and move beyond boss, manager, or decision maker. To be effective in this regard, set goals around growing as a leader. In meetings, how often are you the first person to speak? Do you ask questions, then provide the answer? If you set a goal to become a better listener, thus a better leader, consider how you can do this on a daily basis. Instead of writing "prepare for meeting" on your to-do list, consider writing "develop questions to ask" and "speak last at the meeting." Start shifting from a to-do list to a goals-oriented list. If you think about this from a personal or family standpoint, you may want to raise well-adjusted, kind children. What steps are you taking to do this? How will you accomplish this goal? Just stating it out loud but never actually taking the steps or initiative to make it happen will have the same outcome as wanting to lose 20 pounds but not taking action. The weight does not just fall off, and your kids will not turn out the way you hoped simply because you *wanted* it to happen. Set a goal to have conversations with your children about acts of kindness or respect. Make it a goal to ask your children how they will respond to a setback after one occurs.

BE WARY OF THE PLANNING FALLACY: Nothing happens in the time we think it will. We are all guilty of believing we will get the task done in the time we set aside but it rarely happens for a multitude of reasons. We can get interrupted if we do not block off the time. It turns out we might need to do more research before we can finish the project or reply to the colleague. It does not just happen at work, and when it happens at home, the impact can be felt even more. The amount of time to plan and prep dinner or to get multiple kids dressed and out of the house almost always takes longer than you expect. In our life, we only get so much time with those who are important to us and we also have to take care of certain tasks as adults: mowing the lawn, taking out the trash, doing the dishes. Be sure to set a schedule, and allow room for error to ensure you do not miss out on time with your loved ones. Stick to the schedule as well. Broken promises lead to distrust, and there is very little that can damage a relationship more than a lack of trust.

USE THE FLYWHEEL EFFECT: Take steps every day towards your goals and do not allow external events or circumstances to get in the way of those steps. Each day that we make progress is a day we are closer to our goals or dreams. The days you do not want to get out of bed to go to the gym or finish an assignment for the online class you are taking are the most important days to forge ahead. When you move forward each day, you will build momentum. This momentum has the ability to result in the flywheel effect. Collins talks about the effort it would require to push a 5,000 pound flywheel. After hours and hours of hard work, you get the wheel to rotate once, then twice and so on until, eventually, it is spinning on its own. As the flywheel rotates, someone comes along and asks you, "Which push got it going so fast?" You think about it and realize you have no idea. Was it the very first push that got it started or the 100th? Was it the 1,000th when you felt like you got some momentum? The reality is that the consistent effort and pressure you put forth resulted in the spinning of the flywheel. This is the same as our daily commitments to meeting our goals. We have to be comfortable with incremental steps that get us to where we want to be.

EXPERIENCE + REFLECTION = LEARNING AND PROGRESS: In his famous last lecture, Randy Pausch stated, "Experience is what you get when you *didn't* get what you wanted. And experience is often the most valuable thing you have to offer." We all receive the gift of experience every day; what we do with that is what matters. When we set aside the time to reflect on the experience and consider how we can use it to move forward, we are making progress in our growth and development as a person. If we learn nothing from the experience, it is as if it never happened. We have to remember that although we often want to share with others, not everyone is ready to learn from someone else's experience. Before we try to pass it on, we have to sit with it, reflect on it and identify what we learned from it. Every morning after my workout routine, I take the time to reflect on the previous day's events. I consider interactions at work and at home. I reflect on choices I made and what I could have done differently. I think about what was said in a meeting and if it was helpful or harmful. I reflect on whether the experience with a colleague helped strengthen our relationship or if I made choices that damaged the relationship. Was I reactionary in the moment, or did I take the time to detach and respond in a meaningful manner? This quiet reflection time helps to set the table for the day. It is humbling at times and can even be painful. To help offset that feeling, I end with the same question: What three things am I grateful for today? This is a reminder that even if I made mistakes or was not the leader/parent/spouse I hoped to be, I still have plenty to be grateful for in my life including the opportunity to get better tomorrow.

EVERY CHALLENGE IS AN OPPORTUNITY AND A CASE STUDY FOR FUTURE CHALLENGES: Our mindset and approach to life directly impacts what happens next. When we sulk and wallow in self-pity because life gets hard or something happened that is out of our control, we are heading down a hole. Each challenge we face in life, no matter how big or how small, is an opportunity for us to grow and move forward. You cannot choose the cards you are dealt, but you always have a choice in how you play those cards. It is a test of our commitment to life and to those around us. As we evaluate the opportunity and see what we can learn, we are developing a path to help us in the future. We use the experience + the reflection to know how to accept the opportunity and navigate it the next time we find ourselves in a similar situation. As you engage in the opportunity, stop and ask yourself:

- What can I learn?
- How can I grow?
- How will this make me stronger?

These questions will propel you upward as opposed to thoughts such as, "Why is this happening to me?" that pull you downward. There are any number of situations I could reference as a school leader whether it involves students, faculty, or parents. The beauty of working in schools is that each day brings a new set of challenges and opportunities. The most difficult conversations with a faculty member are learning opportunities for the next conversation with that same faculty member or maybe another. By reflecting on how you handled the situation, you are better prepared for the future.

ASK – WHAT IS THE BEST THING THAT CAN HAPPEN:

Too often in life, when presented with opportunities, we stop and begin to think about everything that can go wrong if we say yes. We seek reasons why we should not say yes to the opportunity or take the first step in a new direction. It forces us to pause and wait; potentially, resulting in us missing out on the opportunity. We can then make an excuse that it was not the right timing, or it would not have worked out anyway. We are back to drifting in life instead of taking action.

To be clear, when we do nothing, we are still making a choice, and there are consequences. To clarify, I do not suggest jumping headfirst into every opportunity that comes your way. Take time to think and reflect as well as have conversations with people in your life. However, the focus should remain positive and continue to look at the best outcome. When we start with the question, "What is the best thing that can happen?" the opportunities and outcomes become limitless. We might get the raise or the promotion. She might accept the offer on the house. He might say yes to my proposal. If we are looking at all of the positive outcomes, we are more likely to take the risk, and there is very little reward in life without risk. If we only think about everything that can go wrong, we talk ourselves out of applying for that promotion, and we let self-doubt creep into our minds. This becomes an ongoing issue because a lack of confidence will keep you from taking risks and living the life you are capable of living. There is an ongoing cycle between confidence and success. We can argue about which comes first, but at the end of the day, each one will result in more of the other. Nothing in life is guaranteed and a positive outlook may not result in the outcome you hoped, but failing to take action and always looking from a pessimistic point of view will certainly result in long term failure. As Henry Ford said, "Whether you think you can or think you can't – you're right."

FOCUS ON WHAT YOU CAN CONTROL – YOUR EFFORT AND YOUR ATTITUDE: Only one person has control over your effort and your attitude - you. Depending on your situation you may or may not have control of what is happening each day at home or at work. In fact, there are some daily aspects of life that we will never have control over. For example, traffic. I do not know what traffic will look like each day when I leave my house, but I have 100% control over when I leave my house and the route I take to work. It is with this mindset and approach that we can begin to recognize what is out of our control and focus on what is in our control. Every morning, I am up at 4:30 to work out, which includes either a run or bike ride. I have no control over the weather in the morning, but I can be prepared by checking the weather the night before and determining what clothes I should wear or if I need to exercise indoors. By planning ahead, I approach my workout with the right attitude. Similarly, I have no control over what the day will bring when I arrive at school, but I do know, as a leader within a school, no two days are alike. I can build my daily schedule to allow for emergencies and focused work time. By planning ahead and thinking about the future, I am better prepared to take control of my attitude. Once I begin to take control of this aspect of my life, I can focus on my effort. Hall of Fame UCLA Basketball Coach, John Wooden, used to tell his players, "Give me 100%. You can't make up for a poor effort today by giving 110% tomorrow. You don't have 110%. You only have 100%, and that's what I want from you right now." This is an incredibly important message for all of us and for our teams at home, in the office and throughout our life. Each of us is an integral part of a team in some way or fashion, and our teammates deserve our best. How you approach the day is entirely up to you, but it will have a lasting impact on your success in life. As we approach our day and find ourselves less than excited about a task or assignment at the office, we can still put in our best effort. No one else has control over the effort you put in regardless of the assignment given to you. The moment you start letting other people impact your effort and attitude, that is the moment you start losing the day. Maintaining the right approach requires conscious effort and intentionality on your part.

MAKE INFORMED DECISIONS – ACT ON THOSE DECISIONS: In most cases leaders have access to all of the information needed to make decisions. We may not have every detail that we want, but after reviewing what is available and contemplating the information you have, be decisive and make a decision. Every hour, day or week that goes by that you sit on a decision, it becomes harder to make. If you cannot fully commit to a decision, take a step in the direction you think is right. After you do this, evaluate if it was correct or not, then make the next decision to either continue forward or pivot. Think about using the map on your phone when you are in a new city. You step out of the hotel to go to a restaurant and the map is spinning because it does not have its bearings yet. You can stand there waiting or you can start walking. As soon as you start walking and the map realizes where you are, it will let you know if you are heading in the right direction or if you need to stop and change direction. The only reason you are now headed in the right direction is because you took action. Changing your mind or making a different decision once you have more information is not flip-flopping, it is making an informed decision with newly acquired information. This is something to talk with your colleagues or faculty about. When our administrative team makes a decision that impacts our faculty, I relay the information we used to make the decision and why it was made. We then talk about how to implement it and move forward. Everyone is not always in agreement, but having the knowledge of how a decision was reached and how to move forward is always helpful.

BE ASSERTIVE – CHOOSING NOT TO ACT IS STILL A CHOICE: It is easy to put off a decision that you know is difficult to make, especially if you are concerned about how it will impact others. The decision not to do anything is still a choice, and you have to recognize and own that. Every school leader has been faced with a difficult decision of how to move forward in a way that is best for the students, the school, and the community. If we put off the decision and choose not to act, there are consequences. These can range in complexity, depending on the actual concern, but the longer you wait to act, the more damage can occur and the more difficult it might be to act in the future. Consider your options, consult mental models or consider past experiences, and make a decision. One suggested mental model is to use second order principles. If I make *this* choice, then *that* will happen. Look forward and be prepared for the outcome, whatever your choice.

USE MENTAL MODELS TO UNDERSTAND PROBLEMS AND MAKE DECISIONS: Some decisions are more difficult and will have a greater impact than others. In those cases, you may want to take more time and consider utilizing mental models. We unconsciously use mental models every day, and we should be intentional in using them for larger decisions. I encourage you to take advantage of the information out there to help you understand problems and make decisions. Shane Parrish and his team at Farnam Street have a fantastic list that you can reference whenever you need it. When you start using second order thinking, you go deeper in your thought process and think beyond the immediate outcomes of your decisions.

If you contemplate Hanlon's Razor (another mental model), you see the bias that exists when you bring past experiences into your work with an employee or colleague that you do not always work well with on projects. We will dig deeper into these models later in the book.

LOOK FOR BOTH POSITIVE AND NEGATIVE PATTERNS – HOW CAN YOU BUILD MORE POSITIVE EXPERIENCES AND LIMIT THE NEGATIVE: There are patterns all throughout our lives, but we are often too busy to notice them until it is too late, and we end up in a negative space physically or emotionally. Daily and weekly reflections will help you identify some of the patterns that exist in our lives. Each night before you go to bed or each morning after you wake up, spend some time reflecting on the day in a journal. We all need to use a model that works for us, and I have tried several over the years. Currently, I ask myself four questions that help me see these patterns and reflect on what I need to do.

- What win(s) did I have today?
- What lessons did I learn today?
- What are the next steps I need to take?
- What am I grateful for?

Each of these questions provides me with insight into what is happening in my life. If I do not take the time to visit with myself and consider these questions, I am drifting and simply reacting each day to what is happening in my life. By focusing on these questions, I am taking an active role in my life and I am identifying patterns.

I see how the patterns are connected to my habits and choices. I also see connections to past experiences. I note situations in which I become frustrated or lose my temper and make comments I regret when speaking to colleagues or loved ones. For example, when I am feeling stress, I often become terse or short in my responses. It is my way of trying to signal to folks that I am stressed and do not have time to respond. This does not create a positive experience for others nor am I helping the situation. Instead, I should respond with the fact I am feeling stress about another topic and do not believe I can give the adequate or necessary time to the question or situation. I encourage you to consider a specific cue that you can identify, and recognize how to step back, detach and avoid the negative path. The same is true for decisions around health. If you drink alcohol, are there times when you consume more than you should? Is it tied to stress at work or at home? What is the result of you having more than you should? Did the occasional happy hour turn into the weekly or daily? If so, why? Spend time looking for patterns of positive behavior, of when you are your best. What do those experiences have in common? Is it the people you are around? Is it tied to an aspect of work or a hobby? How can you build more of these positive experiences into your daily life so you can limit the negative experiences? This is about detaching and looking at choices you are making and developing the discipline to focus on the opportunities for more positive experiences.

DO NOT FOCUS ON THE PAST: We all have regrets in life and wish we may have done or said something different. We also know that we cannot go back and make changes to what happened. The events of the past are gone, and the time you put into thinking about it is time you lose. Yes, we should reflect and consider lessons learned, but then we need to move forward. Dwelling on the past keeps us from having the ability to move forward with our lives. It prevents us from taking risks or engaging with certain people because we are afraid of what might happen, especially when the past experience is a negative one. Likewise, you may have had a wonderful event occur in the past that you like to refer back to, but if we spend too much time celebrating the past, we miss the present, and the future will not be what we want. Each day provides a new opportunity for you to learn and grow in a way that will help you move forward in your relationships with yourself and others. This is not possible if we worry about what happened. Socrates stated, "The secret of change is to focus all of your energy, not on fighting the old but on building the new." This is an approach teachers bring with them each day to the classroom. There is an opportunity to create an entirely new experience for your students, regardless of the previous day's lesson.

DO NOT LET NEGATIVE PEOPLE OR NEGATIVE EXPERIENCES RENT SPACE IN YOUR HEAD: Similar to focusing on past experiences, we sometimes allow ourselves to focus on negative interactions or negative people in our lives. We all have interactions with people that are not positive. This can be a general attitude on their part, or it can be part of the baggage that exists in your relationship with that person. In his book, *Originals: How Non-Conformists Move the World*, Adam Grant talks about ambivalent relationships or frenemies. According to Grant, "Negative relationships are unpleasant, but they're predictable: if a colleague consistently undermines you, you can keep your distance and expect the worst." It can be easier to push this person out of your head because you clearly recognize the negative experience. Grant goes on to say, "But when you're dealing with ambivalent relationships, you're constantly on guard, grappling with questions about when the person can actually be trusted." He then shares a comment from Michelle Duffy, "It takes more emotional energy and coping resources to deal with individuals who are inconsistent." These are the individuals who take up a lot of space in our head from the continuous grappling. If the experiences and relationship tend to be negative, work to keep them from renting space in your head. It takes effort, going back and forth trying to determine if the experience is going to be positive or negative, if the person has my best interest in mind or is being manipulative. If the relationship requires that much effort, you should move on. Your energy should be focused on building and maintaining more positive relationships. This will fill you with greater joy, purpose, and happiness.

BE GRATEFUL: This is an action and a choice. We hear the suggestion often: *you should be more grateful*, but many people do not act on the suggestion or live with an attitude of gratitude. In *Evolving With Gratitude: Small Practices in Learning Communities That Make a Big Difference with Kids, Peers, and the World*, Lainie Rowell states, "In difficult times, I've tried it both ways - living with a grateful disposition OR focusing on the negative things I can't control. It's my experience that one feels much better than the other, offering me resiliency and hope." This disposition, or approach to life, extends beyond stating your appreciation and saying thank you because you feel an obligation. The statements of gratitude need to be genuine, and you have to believe it. You can take additional steps in the right direction towards being grateful by recognizing your faculty or family and sharing how much you appreciate their role in your life. Developing a grateful mindset takes work and practice; it will not just happen. After hearing about a gratitude journal for years, even mocking the idea, I have been writing in a journal every morning since the spring of 2017, and it always ends with the same question: What am I grateful for today? It forces me to pause and think about all that I have in my life and all that I should be grateful for. This might be about my family or about someone at work that helped on a project. By stopping what you are doing each day to acknowledge what you have in life, you start to appreciate what you have; you become more grateful. It starts to become ingrained in your life resulting in a more positive attitude and happier existence. You do not find yourself wanting more but rather appreciating what you have and those around you. Greg McKeown, author of *Essentialism: The Disciplined Pursuit of Less* and *Effortless: Make It Easier to Do What Matters Most*, states, "When you focus on what you lack, you lose what you have. When you focus on what you have, you gain what you lack."

LET EVERYONE IN YOUR LIFE WHO MATTERS KNOW THAT THEY MATTER: Our time together is finite, yet we make choices as if we will live forever. As Confucius says, "You have two lives. The second one begins when you realize you only have one." We delay calls to loved ones and trips with family. We tell ourselves, there will be another time for it or it can wait until later. Over 7,000 people die every day in the US, and you can be certain many of them expected to wake up the next day. It is likely they chose to put something off for another day only to miss the opportunity because there was no tomorrow for them. Let's look at a more optimistic approach, and say I will live to the average lifespan of 79 years. As morbid as it may be, I can easily determine how many days I have left to share with loved ones and people who matter in my life. At 45 years old, I have less than

13,000 days left to live. That sounds like a lot, but when you factor in some non-negotiables like sleep, the number of days decreases as I am not awake during some of those hours to make the most of my time. This may seem like a pessimistic or negative way to look at your life, but it is really just a realistic viewpoint and one that should help you remember the importance of telling people how you feel about them. You should think about all of the good you can do today for the world and for those around you. No one is promised tomorrow.

BE HAPPY FOR OTHERS – SHARE HAPPINESS AND JOY WHENEVER POSSIBLE: As we work to build more gratitude into our daily life, we are able to take this next step. It can be difficult because the idea of celebrating or being happy for others goes against much of what we see and hear all around us every day. Our society and culture depicts a message that we should be fighting for what is ours, and everything is a competition with clear winners and losers. In addition to that, if you do not win, you should be mad, angry or jealous of the victor. This does not encourage personal growth or development. The only competition that matters is the one with yourself. Are you a better version of yourself today than you were yesterday, last week, last month, last year? When you spend less time worrying about what others have or what you don't have, there is more room in your life for gratitude and appreciation. You can develop the ability to be happy for someone else.

> Make it a habit to participate in the German practice of **mitfreude**, wishing goodwill towards others and the Sanskrit **muditā**, being happy for the accomplishment of others.

> *"Hard choices, easy life.
> Easy choices, hard life."*
> *–Jerzy Gregorek*

We have choices every day in how we respond to our environment and what is happening around us. If we do not prepare for these events, we are not going to move forward or improve. We also cannot respond appropriately if we do not know our why. Each individual must be able to identify their why, or purpose, as that is what will drive you to get up each morning and bring yourself to the world. The next step in your preparation is to develop a set of principles and standards that guide you. Once you establish your standards, you will be prepared for the unexpected and find an opportunity to grow through the challenge or setback. You will recognize areas to focus such as your effort and attitude. Consider your approach to decision making and ways to strengthen it by developing an understanding of mental models and the importance of taking incremental steps. These principles will generate clarity and also help you develop a stronger appreciation for the world around you - a sense of gratitude. Once you develop this, you will recognize that you likely have all that you need.

EXAMPLE:

PRINCIPLE: Focus on what you can control, your effort and your attitude.

WHAT I DID BEFORE: I made excuses or pointed the finger at others when my input or suggestions were not included in the decision making process. I created stories in my head for why the other team members were looked at more favorably. I looked to cast blame when I found myself in a difficult or frustrating situation.

WHAT I WANT TO DO DIFFERENTLY: I will honestly evaluate the effort and contributions I am making to my team. I will seek feedback to determine how objective my own observations are regarding both. I will view the work of my colleagues and team members in a positive light with the understanding that we are all working to achieve the mission. I will reflect on what I can do differently and how I can improve.

HOW WILL I ACCOMPLISH THIS: I will begin to journal daily with a few simple prompts or questions: How did I positively contribute to the team and mission today? Did I bring my best self to the office today? What can I do differently tomorrow? These questions will have you thinking about your effort and attitude on a daily basis. You will see patterns that you can address, and make the improvements you are seeking.

QUESTIONS TO CONSIDER:

- Do you have a list of core values you live by?
- Are there standards you hold yourself to on a daily or weekly basis?
- Do you know your why?
- Are you making choices that help or hinder your growth?

CHAPTER 2
RELATIONSHIP PRINCIPLES

Successful leaders have the ability to build and strengthen relationships. This requires constant attention and care by the leader. Each interaction you have with your team ends with you adding to or subtracting from the relationship. We do not simply maintain a relationship because if we are not tending to it, the relationship is getting weaker by the day. You may not use each of these principles every day or in every interaction but some, such as listening, require your daily attention. Each of the principles listed below will help you develop as a person, professionally and personally.

> *The importance of **listening** cannot be overemphasized in any relationship.*

LISTEN BEFORE YOU TALK: We are social beings and part of that involves communicating with each other. The challenge is that everyone has an opinion and wants to share it at a meeting or in a conversation. Unfortunately, the opposite is not true. Not everyone chooses to listen when engaged in a conversation. In order to communicate effectively though, each person needs to know what the other person is thinking or feeling so there can be an appropriate exchange of ideas. Without this, we are just talking at each other, or worse, talking over each other. Too often, individuals are simply waiting their turn to respond instead of listening to what the other person is saying. This is a skill that requires daily practice and being present. You can ask clarifying questions that provide you with additional information. You can restate the person's comments to ensure you understand the message. There are multiple ways to engage in a meaningful conversation through active listening without speaking your mind. At work, there are numerous conversations throughout the day as you are engaging with peers, bosses and those who work directly under your supervision (direct reports). To better facilitate a conversation, listen first, ask questions and speak last. The moment you begin talking, the other person's ability to provide you with information comes to an end. If one of your teachers has a concern and, rather than asking questions and listening, you begin explaining away their concern, the conversation is essentially over; you have lost their support. You ended it by taking away their voice. Instead, provide space for people to express how they are feeling about the work they are doing or how the team is doing. This is also true when talking to your boss. Listen to what they tell you, and respond accordingly with clarifying questions before you begin to make excuses or try to dismiss the concern. In order to provide the best response, you need to hear everything the boss has to say. In marriage, you owe it to your spouse to listen to what they say and are feeling. That relationship is built on mutual respect, trust and love. None of that exists if you do all of the talking and only value your own opinion. When having mundane conversations such as what to prepare for dinner or what restaurant to choose, ask your spouse for their opinion. Engage in a conversation about the topic and ask questions, especially if you do not agree. Develop an understanding of the other person's thought process in the moment and most importantly, listen.

LISTEN TO UNDERSTAND: After taking an important step of recognizing why we need to listen before we speak, we now must listen to understand. We do this through active listening that includes asking clarifying questions. We can take notes so we are able to recall what has been shared in the event it is a presentation or lengthy statement. Our phone and computer should be out of sight so as not to create any distractions. In a 2018 Harvard Business Review article, authors Kristin Duke, Adrian Ward, Aylet Gneezy, and Maarten Bos shared the results of a study on the impact of your phone being visible,

> Having your cell phone nearby takes a toll on your thinking. In two lab experiments, nearly 800 people completed tasks designed to measure their cognitive capacity. Before completing these tasks, the researchers asked participants to either: place their phones in front of them (face-down on their desks), keep them in their pockets or bags, or leave them in another room. The results were striking: the closer the phone to the participant, the worse they fared on the task. The mere presence of our smartphones is like the sound of our names or a crying baby – something that automatically exerts a gravitational pull on our attention. Resisting that pull takes a cognitive toll.

When your mind begins to wander to another topic or create a response, refocus on the person speaking. If you fail to do so, you are not listening and instead just waiting for your turn in the conversation to speak. This is the equivalent of ignoring the person's comments, questions, or thoughts. Simply responding without understanding what the other person needs, demonstrates a lack of empathy or willingness to listen. If one of your teachers stops by the office with a concern about a colleague or student, they want you to understand why this is a challenge or a problem for them. They do not want a simple response that attempts to fix the problem for them. When we give advice or offer to fix a problem, it can appear as if we gave no thought to the concern and just wanted to provide an answer so they would leave. Also, if we become problem-solvers for our faculty, they will not learn how to solve problems for themselves. I always remind teachers at the beginning of the year about the importance of putting out small fires on their own in the classroom. This gives them ownership in their classroom and strengthens their relationship with students. Instead of trying to fix their problems, ask clarifying questions that will help you understand the issue but also get the teacher thinking about the problem in a different way. Some questions might include:

- Has this happened before?
- What strategies work with this student?
- What strategies have not worked?

When we listen to understand, we help the other person in the conversation, not just ourselves. Look back at the example of dinner plans with your spouse. When they make a recommendation and you simply counter with another option, you did not listen to understand, you just waited for your turn. Perhaps the idea stems from a recent recommendation or what the person had for lunch. There can be any number of reasons for the way they feel, and you miss the chance to learn when you just give your opinion in response. Listening to understand might be most important when serving in the role of a parent. When your child wakes you up in the middle of the night because they do not feel well or had a bad dream, they simply want to be heard and know that you care. You have to ask clarifying questions, not incredibly deep, philosophical questions but simple questions like where does it hurt? What does the pain feel like? If instead, you just tell them it will be okay, go back to bed, you missed an opportunity. This shows a lack of care and empathy when they are in a highly vulnerable state.

RESPOND – DO NOT REACT: We have learned, over millennia, to react to our environment. Our fight or flight response has been honed for generations, even though the danger no longer comes from a hungry animal tracking us in the wilderness. Instead, we may react similarly to a comment at a board meeting, email from a parent, or rejection. In Kate Murphy's book, *You're Not Listening: What You're Missing and Why It Matters*, she references the work of Ahmad Hariri at Duke University. He studies the amygdala which governs our fight or flight response. If we do not learn how to engage our brain with the appropriate level of response, we are at the mercy of our evolutionary path and primitive brain, which results in us reacting to the moment. This can show up through raised voices, eye rolling and angry email or text responses that we later regret. This happens every time we react to our environment as opposed to responding to our environment. While our decisions may not be in the same realm as a fighter pilot, we can take a lesson from United States Air Force Colonel, John Boyd, and his OODA Loop theory: Observe, Orient, Decide, Act. Fighter pilots have to make decisions within seconds when flying against an enemy combatant. If they just reacted without taking a moment to engage in the OODA Loop, it could have deadly consequences.

Unlike fighter pilots who are making split-second decisions, we have the luxury of extending the time to consider our response and should effectively utilize the OODA Loop. Working in education, we are often confronted with difficult situations either with students, parents, or even faculty members. If a student comes to see you, upset about their performance on an assessment and is blaming the teacher, what is your reaction or the tone you take with them? The first reaction may be to put the blame back on the student for not adequately preparing for the assessment or perhaps questioning the student's commitment to the course. Instead, ask questions (observe) and develop an understanding (orient) about what happened. Then, respond (decide/act) accordingly. The student may not have given the assessment the attention it deserved, and if you respond in a way that helps them reach this discovery on their own instead of casting blame, they are more likely to learn the lesson. Another example at work might involve a conversation around the budget. The Head of School states the budget numbers are off, and we need to identify areas to make cuts. Your immediate reaction may be to blame another colleague or another department for the shortfall. Before you take that step, detach and use the moment to think (observe and orient) about what they are asking of you and respond (decide and act) with thoughtful, clarifying questions. Gather information (observe and orient) during the conversation, and determine the best course of action (decide and act). Looking ahead, you might be the one getting negative feedback or questions from your team after the cuts and will once again need to identify a way to respond, not react.

ASK QUESTIONS – SHOW GENUINE CURIOSITY: Individuals who possess strong listening skills are curious and ask questions. Leaders have too few models of this today, and the typical conversation they observe is nothing more than verbal ping pong. We see people talking at each other instead of to each other. We observe individuals share opinions without considering the other person's point of view and often only hear what they want to hear. This is not actually listening, nor is it a conversation. One way to encourage yourself to develop better listening skills is to be thoughtful and ask meaningful questions that are important to the other person in the conversation. For example:

- Can you share more?
- How did that make you feel?
- What do you see as the challenge here?

When you are engaging with another person and asking questions, they feel a connection to you and it builds trust. If a teacher comes to you complaining about a colleague or the department chair, it is your role to help them process it with genuine questions.

- "Can you share more background information?"
- "Has this happened before?"
- "How can I support you here?"

As a leader, it is not your job to solve problems for people but to help them find their own solutions. We can do this by asking the right questions. All of this takes practice and you can do this at home as well. When your spouse comes home and you ask the mundane, "How was your day," are you really just asking because you feel like you're supposed to? We should shift our questions to be more caring and inquisitive.

- "Did anything exciting happen at work today?"
- "How did you feel at work today?"
- "Did you have any wins today?"

If your spouse responds that it was a tough or challenging day, try following up with "What do you need from me tonight?" This demonstrates empathy and a commitment to the relationship. We have a choice every day to either work on building our relationships up or tearing them down. Being curious and asking thoughtful questions will strengthen your relationships.

BE RESPECTFUL: It is disappointing to see how little respect we see today when we stop to observe what is happening around us. Please and thank you are not just empty platitudes, they are meaningful comments that keep the foundation of personal relationships stable. Use them consistently and be authentic in your appreciation.

Our own opinion and experience seem to be all that matters in conversations and decision making. With this mindset, disagreements shift easily to arguments. It is important for us to acknowledge that everyone will not always agree, and that is okay. Some of the best ideas or recommendations arise from differing viewpoints. That can only happen, though, if there is mutual respect between parties. Acknowledge the other person's thoughts or ideas, and see how they align or do not align with your own. Listen to understand. If the disagreement is a point of contention after the meeting, find a way to leave it there. Do not bring that feeling with you to a future meeting and openly discuss it with others. It is disrespectful to everyone involved. First, it is disrespectful to the individual from the previous meeting. They are not airing the dirty laundry from your meeting, nor should you. Second, it is disrespectful to those in the next meeting because you are taking away their time with you. As the leader in an organization, be respectful of everyone's time and opinion.

ADMIT WHEN YOU ARE WRONG AND BE CAREFUL NOT TO ACCUSE OTHERS OF BEING WRONG: This is one of the most important things a leader can do as it shows a level of accountability that most individuals do not have or do not want to have. Every leader has made a mistake and will make more mistakes in the future.

We cannot have a culture of accountability in our organization or school if we do not admit when we make mistakes. It does not need to be a special meeting, nor does there need to be a lengthy explanation. Simply state to the group or person affected that you made a mistake. You should also share how you plan to address it as well as avoid it in the future. If you wronged a colleague or employee in a meeting, you should apologize to the person privately, and also let them know you plan to apologize to the team. They should have an opportunity to express their feelings with regard to your group apology. It may be as simple as telling the group you want to apologize for your behavior and that you already apologized to the person affected. The level of detail you get into with the team will depend on how comfortable the person is who received the apology. Similarly, you want to be conscious of the conversations you have with employees when they make a mistake. Unless there is a true danger of the individual's decision having a large-scale impact on the company or organization, there may be little to no benefit in telling that person they are wrong. You are better off asking specific questions that help the individual reach that conclusion on their own. If you can develop an organization that has people accepting responsibility and admitting when they are wrong or make mistakes, you will have an incredibly strong organization that people will not want to leave. This starts and ends with the leader modeling the behavior. One of the biggest lessons you can give a person is telling them when you made a mistake or are wrong, especially if it impacts them. You should set the example for others in your life.

KNOW YOUR ROLE IN EVERY SITUATION: There are leaders and followers in every situation. Likewise, there are learners and knowers in every situation. Take the time to stop and reflect on this prior to a meeting or a conversation so you are able to contribute in a meaningful way. There are times when we forget our role in the meeting because the topic is of interest or we are invested in the outcome. When you are in that situation and feel yourself becoming increasingly engaged or perhaps irritated by the direction of the meeting, detach and look around. It may help to physically push your chair away from the table to focus your mind on the task of detaching. Take stock of what is happening, and recall what your role is and how to best serve in that role. You may have a leadership role due to your title, but that does not mean you are always in charge, always have the answers or always serve as the leader in the room. Take the time to prepare for meetings and conversations in your organization. Go into them with the knowledge of your role. The Board Chair might be in the room, but you have the floor for the presentation and are, therefore, the leader in that moment. When questions arise, you may also be the knower who has important information. Be humble in this moment, and acknowledge the other leaders and knowers in the room who can contribute to the discussion. Likewise, identify the time to defer at team meetings when your direct reports are presenting a plan. Be curious and ask questions. Listen to what is being shared, and fill the role of learner. All of these roles are interchangeable on a daily basis. Develop the self-awareness to know your role. Remember that great leaders start out as great followers. The strongest leaders understand what it takes to be a great follower and do what they can to help them be their best. As a parent, I am looked to as a leader by my children, but that does not mean I know everything. Let your children know that you are learning with them, whether that is math homework, playing an instrument or even going on a hike. We should always be seeking to learn more and model this for everyone in our lives, young and old.

BE HONEST AND TRANSPARENT WITH PEOPLE IN YOUR LIFE: The poem *The Man in the Glass,* by (Peter) Dale Winbrow, Sr., hangs in my office directly above my computer so I can see it every day. I do not read it often enough, but it is there to remind me of the importance of honesty and transparency. Relationships are built on trust, and trust is earned through honest and transparent communication. To be clear, there are levels of this, and understanding that is important. There is a false narrative that we need to provide all of the information we have all of the time, but that is not the case. Your team does need to know what is happening and what you are thinking in every situation. There is a dichotomy though, and you should not intentionally keep people in the dark. You should share the information you have or information that is not confidential. Follow that up by telling your team that is all you can share at this time. For example, you may not be able to tell your team the exact details of why someone had to be let go. You should not lie and say they resigned or simply ignore the fact that it happened and hope people do not notice. Instead, you can tell them that you had to make a difficult personnel decision and, while the details are confidential, no one else is being let go. If that changes for some reason, you will notify them. If there is a budgetary issue, you should not lie and say everything is going to be okay if there are legitimate concerns. Instead, state that the budget is an area of concern, and strategies need to be identified for hitting the numbers this quarter or there will be changes. Ask them to meet the next day to start laying out a strategy. That last statement gives ownership and agency while still being honest and transparent. This can happen at home as well when your child asks if they are smart or if you think they are a good basketball player. You should not lie to your child, but you also may not be completely honest. You might talk about areas to grow or develop as a player, and introduce them to the importance of a growth mindset and deliberate practice. Being honest and transparent means you do not lie or conceal the truth, but it can be nuanced in some circumstances.

IDENTIFY PROBLEMS EARLY ON AND ADDRESS THEM: Too often, we do not look to identify problems but wait for them to come to us. This is due, in part, to our desire to focus on the positives and find ways to expand them. If we are being honest, sometimes we choose to avoid the work that is required to address the problem. After all, once you identify the problem, you need to address it, and that takes time and energy. It may also require some introspection to see if you are part of the problem. The longer you delay responding, the bigger the problem will become, and it certainly will not go away just because you ignore it.

SEEK THE ROOT CAUSE – NOT THE ACTION: Once a problem is identified, you must dig in to find the root cause. Too often we stay on the surface and simply look at the outcome. For example, you share the following statement with an employee: "You failed to meet the deadline." While that may be true, we need to find out the cause of the problem:

- Was the deadline not achievable?
- Were adequate resources provided to meet the deadline?
- Is there too much on the individual's plate?

If we do not take the time to identify the root cause, the same outcome or problem will persist. You may see patterns emerge across your organization when you begin to look for the root cause of problems. We ask our teachers to write comments twice a year for their students. Invariably, we run into a time crunch and issues with deadlines. We know it is coming and simply accept it. By stepping back and looking at the root - lack of time, we can take the steps to mitigate the issue. If we provide additional time for teachers to write by having a delayed start to school or early dismissal, we are providing the additional time needed to meet the deadline. This approach allows you to make progress and move forward because you are not reacting to the problem at the surface level. Instead of having to speak with the faculty member at the last minute with a looming deadline, you already took care of the root of the problem: lack of time. If there are still individuals struggling to meet your deadline, repeat the process of identifying the root cause as they may have their own unique challenges outside of school.

HAVE CLEAR EXPECTATIONS FOR OTHERS IN YOUR LIFE AND ALLOW THEM TO HOLD YOU ACCOUNTABLE FOR THEIR EXPECTATIONS OF YOU: In building a team or organization, leaders need to clearly define expectations as well as standards. Whenever possible, allow the team to develop those expectations. If the members of your team or organization hold each other accountable for meeting expectations, you will find far greater success. Your team will move from "the boss says we have to do this," to "we need to do this, let's go." It is a subtle shift, but you can see that ownership is now at play, and that is a large motivator for individuals. When you reach the pinnacle of trust and teamwork, the comments will change to "we get the opportunity to do this, let's get started." Once the team sees opportunities, the work will improve dramatically. In addition, by collaborating on expectations, you allow the team to see your openness to being held accountable. As you become more accountable, you are moving into the role of servant leader, to which we all should aspire. When you enter into a relationship or become a parent, recognize when you must put the needs of others before yourself. There is a balance with this, however. If you always put the needs of others before yourself, you will burn out and not have the ability to help yourself or those around you. Think about the directions you receive on a flight about your oxygen mask. Adults are always told to fix their oxygen mask first before caring for those around them. Share this with the people in your life, and ask them if they are caring for themselves and others. We cannot objectively evaluate ourselves in this way and need feedback from family and friends.

TOUGH LOVE IS NECESSARY AT TIMES – IF YOU PUT COMFORT AHEAD OF SUCCESS, YOU SHOULD EXPECT POOR RESULTS: As a leader, it is imperative to understand how each of your individual team members responds to successes and set-backs. With this knowledge, you can determine how hard to push each one of them to reach their best and to help the team complete the objective. There is an end result that we are all aiming for, regardless of our profession. There are times that we need to put the mission ahead of comfort to ensure we can accomplish it. This is not to say there should never be time to slow down or have comfort; it is simply a recognition that being comfortable all the time will not yield results. There are deadlines that may require longer hours in a given week. There are certain times of the year when your company or organization is busier, and this needs to be acknowledged and accepted. As we emerged from the COVID 19 pandemic, there was a recognition from employers to provide greater compassion and empathy for their employees. There were more conversations around flexibility for employees and working parents. This should have always been the case, yet there are times when certain expectations cannot be compromised. If you are consistent and open with your faculty about the needs of the students and the school, the vast majority of your faculty will understand. Some will even help cover for their colleagues as needed because educators are givers by nature.

MEANINGFUL CONVERSATIONS WILL LEAD TO MEANINGFUL RELATIONSHIPS: A meaningful relationship is an investment. It builds off of meaningful conversations in which you engage the other person in a thoughtful and caring manner. It leads to empathetic conversations and deeper engagement. The more often you have these types of conversations, the more meaning you find in the relationship. There needs to be clarity around your genuine curiosity about their lives, hopes and dreams. There is generally a reciprocity in these conversations as well, and you feel cared for and a part of something bigger than yourself. This requires work and attention. Strong relationships do not just happen; you have to want to build them and invest the time. As a leader of your school or division, be sure to carve out time in your calendar each day for one-on-one check-ins with direct reports. It is unlikely you can meet with everyone in the school, but you can set a model for others to follow. If you are having meaningful conversations with your department chairs, you are modeling the types of conversations they should have with their department members. School leaders need to have conversations with all faculty while also recognizing they will need fellow administrators and leaders to help engage more faculty more often. Be careful not to take any of your relationships for granted. You can look for this by evaluating the types of conversations you are having with individuals. If it is usually a surface-level conversation, then you are not working to develop a relationship with that person or, worse yet, you are allowing it to erode. If the conversation never goes beyond pleasantries, the relationship will not be cultivated. As noted in previous sections, the same is true for your conversations and relationships at home. If you want to connect deeply with your partner or children, you must put in the time. You have to work at the conversations and ensure they always include connection and meaning.

LET EVERYONE IN YOUR LIFE WHO MATTERS KNOW THAT THEY MATTER: We have allowed ourselves to be drawn into our work so deeply that we fail to recognize that the people in our lives are what really matters and the work is secondary. Prior to the pandemic, you could find countless articles on the importance of work-life balance. All of this was turned upside down during the pandemic when many of us were in a lock down and working from home with family members doing the same. As we came out of the pandemic, we needed to seek ways to create work-life harmony. The reality is that there will never be a true balance, and if we learn nothing else from the pandemic, it should be that we stop striving for this mythical balance. To start, balance means there is equal attention paid at all times to all aspects. It is not possible to equally balance your home and work experience on a daily basis. However, harmony allows for a flow where you shift back and forth to what is important and being present in the moment. There are times as a leader in a school that all of your focus and attention must be directed to the student in front of you. Likewise, it is important that you are present at home when having dinner with your family and not splitting time between them and work email. All of the accomplishments at work are often attributed to collaboration and teamwork. Are you acknowledging these people and their efforts? This does not mean there needs to be daily effusive praise, but effort and commitment should be recognized. Our families helped shape us to become the people we are today. Yet too many of us fail to connect with our own parents or siblings on a consistent basis. We have our careers or our own families that keep our attention. There are people who helped you get to where you are today, and they should be acknowledged through your words and actions. Similarly, there are people who help keep you going each day, both at home and at work. We get too comfortable in our relationships at home and start to take people for granted. It is time that you stop, and let your partner know they matter to you and why. Give your children the attention they need to develop and grow into young adults who will acknowledge the people in their lives that matter. Set the example.

HONESTLY EVALUATE THE IDEAS AND OPINIONS OF OTHERS: It is important to enter meetings and conversations assuming best intentions. As Brené Brown states, "I know my life is better when I work from the assumption that everyone is doing the best they can." If we do not take this approach, it is impossible to honestly evaluate the ideas and opinions of others. When we bring our past experience and baggage into a meeting and allow our mind to immediately drift to preconceived negative emotions, we are no longer open to the ideas or suggestions of that person. We close ourselves off and create reasons to oppose the initiative. If we are already thinking, "She doesn't know what she's talking about, her last plan failed," or "He is too young to really know how the system works," there is no reason to even be in the meeting or have the conversation. To clarify, this does not mean you are right and you should cancel the meeting. It also does not mean you always go along with the idea or that you must bring the suggestion of others forward. It *does* mean you should give a fair and honest evaluation because that is what a strong leader always does. Listen to your team, regardless of what has happened previously. If this is difficult, detach and ask yourself if you would think differently about the idea if a colleague you admired had made the suggestion. Back to the ideas of Brené Brown, you must maintain a level of respect for the individual and move beyond what you think of their past work. You should be evaluating each individual idea or suggestion they bring forward and not the person bringing the idea forward. You are aware of people you work with or family members who you often disagree with or hold different opinions than. Differing ideas and thoughts can lead to new ideas and innovation. Embrace this by remaining objective and open to the next great idea. As our world becomes more polarizing, we need to make sure we are focusing on the right areas when evaluating ideas and suggestions from our team.

MOVE FROM BLAME OR CREDIT TO INACCURATE OR ACCURATE: This can be a difficult change to tackle in schools as it requires taking ownership and responsibility for your actions, including those of others. When a parent calls a school leader to share a concern and potentially blame a teacher, it is your role to find out if the statement or concern is accurate or not. In the event it is accurate, you may need to take ownership and accept responsibility for the action. It is possible you were not clear with the teacher about the updated protocol or policy. After acknowledging the concern and determining it was accurate, you then need to speak with the teacher. There are also times when the statement is not accurate, and you will need to work with the parent on identifying why that is the case and how to move forward. When the conversation goes well and the parent offers thanks or praise to you, be careful not to take credit. This is about developing relationships throughout the community, and if we can avoid the idea of blame and credit, we move closer to a partnership. The strongest school relationships are ones where everyone feels a shared responsibility and partnership in the success of the students. The idea of blame is one that many parents deal with at home. A common refrain in households with young children is "he started it" or "it's her fault." As parents we get caught in the middle and will even sometimes feed into this by asking who started it. Instead, we need to ask our children if what their sibling said is accurate or not. We can explain what that means and how to move forward. We can talk about shared responsibility and our roles in the house to ensure a positive environment.

USE OTHER PEOPLE'S IDEAS WHENEVER POSSIBLE – GET BUY-IN: Too many individuals have the false perception that they are the leader because they have all the best ideas. This type of leader will not last long. The reality is that people do not follow ideas; they follow people. They do this because of the relationship you build with them and the genuine interest you show for them as individuals. When you allow your team the autonomy and freedom to make decisions, they respect you more. They know you trust them and have belief in their ability. The problem is that if the idea does not work out, you will be the one taking responsibility. That is scary, especially if there is a boss you have to report to. This is part of developing a strong team and strong relationships. By collaborating and allowing others to run with their ideas, you develop a relationship that leads to accountability and responsibility. This should be part of ongoing conversations with your team. Rather than telling them all the steps that can go wrong along the way, ask them what contingency plans are in place or what options they have considered. They may not have done this and will have to get back to you, or maybe, they will surprise you and have alternative plans already in place. You can ask your team to complete a pre-mortem before putting plans into place. This involves a meeting where you list all of the reasons your plans might fail. Once you develop the list, see what steps can be taken to mitigate the potential issues. Again, the leaders should allow the team to complete this exercise on their own. If you do not trust your people, why are they in the organization in the first place? Do not hire people to micromanage them, hire people to do the job you believe they can do. As Steve Jobs said, "It doesn't make sense to hire smart people and tell them what to do; we hire smart people so they can tell us what to do."

DO NOT JUDGE OTHERS: When we judge people without seeing through their lens, we do not afford ourselves the opportunity to learn. We should be genuinely curious in order to understand differing views. There is knowledge to be gained, and it can be invaluable in decision making. Empathy allows us to see, feel and understand what the other person is experiencing. We must be open to this and suspend judgement. Many school leaders are no longer in the classroom on a daily basis and do not always take the lived experience of a teacher into consideration when making decisions. It is important to detach, and consider their experience before making decisions. The same can be said of the students in your school. Before you consider making a schedule change, be sure to conduct empathy interviews with the stakeholders. Implementing a new program or making a change without considering the viewpoint of others is detrimental to relationships and will result in a negative outcome for all parties including the school leader. Conduct surveys, engage in conversations, and be curious!

This can easily transfer to your home. We may have been children at one time, but we are not experiencing what our children are experiencing in the moment. Yes, we fell off our bike, got into a fight with a friend or had our heart broken, but that does not mean we experienced it in the same way. Be curious and ask questions of your children. Show a true interest in their lives, as opposed to interviewing or, worse yet, interrogating them at the dinner table. Whatever your current position at work and the types of responsibilities you may have had previously, you do not know what people are feeling or experiencing when they come to you. Ask deep questions and listen. Move beyond those stereotypical questions of: "How was your day?" "What grade did you get on your math test?" "What homework do you have tonight?"

Instead, ask questions such as: "What was the best part of your day?" "Did you ask any interesting questions in class today?" "What are you looking forward to tomorrow?" This will foster connection and strengthen your relationship with your children.

PROVIDE FEEDBACK CONSISTENTLY THROUGH COACHING AND SEEK FEEDBACK CONSISTENTLY FROM OTHERS: Feedback allows us to grow, and too many people shy away from it because of the impact it can have when done incorrectly. Speaker and author, Marcus Buckingham, makes an interesting analogy about giving feedback. He equates it with throwing a hand grenade over the fence at someone and then walking to the other side to ask the person how they are doing. While I am sure none of us intend for that to be the case, we do not always consider the type of feedback we give or how we deliver it. The team member should be aware that you intend to deliver feedback either because you ask if they are ready to receive it or you simply inform them that the feedback is needed for a specific reason. Once that is clear, if you just talk at the individual when giving the feedback, they likely will not improve, regardless of whether it is positive or negative. It has to be a conversation, not a lecture. When we think about it from the perspective of coaching, our entire approach can change. As a coach, you want to hold up a mirror for them to see a reflection of the work they are doing or how they are behaving. By taking this approach, you are engaging in a conversation and helping the individual to reflect on the experience. This takes greater time than simply delivering feedback, which is one of the reasons leaders do not practice it. When done properly, coaching happens consistently instead of at quarterly or annual evaluations. It should happen regularly and in the moment, otherwise the opportunity for feedback is lost. As you wrap up a meeting, talk to a colleague or subordinate about how the meeting went, and ask for their impressions. Let them tell you what went well and where they want to see improvements next time. When done well, you may not even have to add additional context or comments. You might just agree and ask some clarifying questions. The benefit of having the conversation right away is that everyone is still in the moment and not having to think back one week, one month or, worst-case scenario, one year. Likewise, ask team members for their impression of a meeting and how you ran it. Seek feedback and coaching so as to model the benefits of it and why it should be embraced. Talk about how you plan to incorporate it into the future.

> **"There is no enjoying the possession of anything valuable unless one has someone to share it with."**
> **– Seneca**

We are a social species and want to belong to a tribe where we feel welcomed and respected. By developing strong relationships at work, home and in our social life, we feel connected. In order to have this feeling, it is important that we focus on several principles. The most important one is listening. By focusing on your teammate, your spouse, or a friend, you are building and strengthening your relationships. Everyone wants to be heard, seen, and valued. By developing stronger listening skills, you will be on the path to building relationships that will last.

Humble leaders are willing to listen and work collaboratively to find solutions. They do not get caught up in who is right or wrong or who deserves credit versus blame. In fact, they acknowledge when they make mistakes and take responsibility on a consistent basis. In addition, leaders who demonstrate empathy make connections and feel closer to team members and family members. They see the challenges and the successes of those around them and engage in meaningful dialogue about both. They provide coaching when needed and seek coaching to model the benefits of it. If you care about developing strong relationships, consider how these principles are reflected in your daily life. Find one or two that you want to address, and make a plan for how you will do it. Establish goals, and seek an accountability partner to help you with those goals.

EXAMPLE:

PRINCIPLE: Listening to understand

WHAT I DID BEFORE: I introduced the meeting agenda and guided the conversations. I typically read the items in order, stated my own opinion on the topic and then asked for input. Depending on my point of view, we either went with my idea or adapted it to someone else's and moved on to the next agenda item.

WHAT I WANT TO DO DIFFERENTLY: I want to begin the meeting with a check in from everyone on the team so they have an opportunity to share out before I speak. I want to read the first item and ask for input before sharing my opinion or thoughts. I want to be the last person to speak and that means I need to get comfortable with silence.

HOW WILL I ACCOMPLISH THIS:

- I will add a note at the top of the agenda about team check-ins to ensure we do not skip this item.
- I will inform the team that I have not done a good job of always listening to their ideas and input. I will then tell them my goal of speaking last after each item (if I need to speak at all) and ask them to hold me accountable.
- I will identify one team member as my accountability partner that I check-in with at the end of each meeting who can provide me with feedback.

QUESTIONS TO CONSIDER:

- Do you listen first and respond second?
- Do you ask genuine questions to better understand the people in your life and the challenges they are facing?
- Who are the most important people in your life?
    - Do they know? Have you told them?
- When entering a conversation, do you assume best intentions?

CHAPTER 3
LEADERSHIP PRINCIPLES

Leadership is a skill that requires daily practice if you wish to be successful. It requires a commitment to certain principles and actions. Each day you have an opportunity to further develop these skills. Any growth or improvement made yesterday does not matter if you do not bring it forward and take more strides today. The people who report to you need your best every day, and implementing these principles in one form or another can help ensure that happens. This list is by no means exhaustive, and there are some days when you will focus on certain principles more than others. I would encourage you to reference this list frequently as a reminder of steps you can take or areas you can focus on to further develop your leadership to help those around you. Your success as a leader should result in greater success and growth for your team. Aim to grow leaders and not followers.

BE HUMBLE: Humility will always carry the day because you recognize there is more to do and more to learn. This is not to say you should not be confident in your abilities or skill set. Confidence in your abilities is necessary for leadership, but the team's ability to see you be humble is what develops followers and future leaders. In his book, *Legacy: What the All Blacks Can Teach Us About the Business of Life*, James Kerr talks about the All Blacks' philosophy of "sweeping the shed." It is part of the rugby team's culture that no single player is bigger than the team and its ancestors. The shed is the name used to describe the locker room, and the All

Blacks make sure the area is cleaner when they leave than it was when they arrived. More importantly, though, you often find the team captain, star players, and coaches leading the process. No one is above sweeping the shed. The comparison to my leadership experience is picking up trash left behind by students at lunch or in the auditorium. It might be cleaning up after a faculty meeting. I must demonstrate leadership through humble acts such as these. This mindset also extends to meetings and conversations with your team. Consider how often you provide space for other team members to speak or present at meetings. Do you acknowledge the work of others and provide public praise? Give credit where it is due, and let people know that you still have more to learn. Talk with others about the steps you take to grow and learn as a leader – what books you are reading, what podcasts or TED Talks you have listened to recently.

MAINTAIN STRATEGIC MISSION – ALLOW FOR TACTICAL CHANGE: These two words (strategy and tactics) get interchanged by people and are not always used accurately. Your strategic mission is your long-term goal. It is the target you wish to reach, and you should not waver in your desire to get there. Your tactics are the steps you take to get to that target. How you get there may change, which makes sense because the world is constantly changing around you. When you lay out the vision, you invariably lay out the steps so everyone on the team can see the path forward. There will be changing conditions around you, and it is important to recognize those changes. You must adapt or adjust accordingly to ensure you reach the target (strategic mission). As a school leader you help set the strategic mission, then allow your team to implement the tactics to reach the vision. They may vary from classroom to classroom, but if we are able to reach our target, we will succeed. By allowing for variation on the way to the target, you are granting autonomy, which helps build trust and demonstrates your humility. If you give specific, step-by-step directions to every team member, you are micromanaging, and that is not a good way to lead. You should think of it the same way as working with your own children. Most people want to raise kind, empathetic, hardworking children. Anyone with more than one child knows that each one is different. The steps needed for one will not be the same as for another. You have to allow for changes in how you interact with and speak to each of your children to help them develop the skill set you want them to have. We are all born with empathy, but it has to be cultivated. There is a reason when one baby starts to cry in a nursery, all the other babies begin to cry. They are showing empathy (Martin and Clark 1982, Sagi and Hoffman 1976, Simner 1971). Be intentional with your kids on how they develop, and show empathy through conversations and actions. The same is true in education and in the classroom. We all want a certain skill set in our students, but each learner is unique, and each teacher also has varying strengths and weaknesses. By knowing the strategic mission and providing for tactical change, we can still reach the desired destination.

KNOW YOUR ROLE IN EVERY SITUATION: We discussed this topic earlier in the relationship principles section and revisit the idea here, within the area of leadership principles. As a leader, people look to you for guidance and clarity. People are watching your body language and paying attention to your tone as well as the language you are using.

Your comments and how you handle a decision are being scrutinized. Be aware of this as you work through a problem with your team. In a room of leaders, defer when appropriate. Allow others to share their thoughts because the more speaking other people do, the more information you are able to gather to strengthen your own idea or, perhaps, to develop a new one. The ability to listen and defer is especially important when you are not the de-facto leader in the room. Your subordinates will take cues from you regarding how you respond to the leadership of others. In essence, you are modeling behavior that you want to see when you are the leader. All good leaders began as good followers. They have the ability to move back and forth between the two roles and know when to do so. Walk into every meeting knowing which setting you are in and what your role is. As a subordinate, you should listen and ask questions of your boss. As the leader, you should listen and ask questions of your team. In either scenario, you will develop a sense of clarity throughout the conversation. When it comes time for the decision making, you will know where you stand and if you are the one making a suggestion or making the final decision based on your role.

THE RIGHT TO SHARE AN IDEA IS NOT THE SAME AS THE RIGHT TO MAKE A DECISION: Good leaders are clear with their team about the objective or goal of the meeting and how decisions will be made. In general, you should consider three options for decision making and explain them each time a discussion ensues that will end with a decision.

> **1) CONSENSUS**: Share with the team how everyone will work together to reach a decision. Welcome dissent, and allow for a devil's advocate. You may

need to be ready to end the conversation with some folks agreeing to disagree. State the final decision and ensure everyone can articulate the how and why behind it prior to leaving the room.

2) DELEGATE: Clearly identify the person who has the expertise to make the decision and share that with the group. Be clear in what you are looking for from the decision maker. The individual will report back to you as the leader with their decision as well as the how and why. Assuming you are in agreement (that should be the case 99% of the time, or you failed to provide accurate info), allow this person to share with the group.

3) TOP-DOWN: As the leader you are taking the full responsibility for making the decision. You should still engage in conversation and gather information from your team. The decision should not be made prior, and it is important you have an open mind. Be curious, and ask clarifying questions of your team. Thank everyone for participating, and share the final decision either in the moment or within an agreed upon time frame.

Be transparent and clear with the team about the process, and explain why you are selecting one of the three options for decision making. One example that comes to mind for decision making in schools is around hiring. An argument can be made for utilizing each of these models depending on the position you are hiring for in your school. If you are hiring a math teacher, you may give the department chair the responsibility, but if you are hiring a college counselor you may want to take on that role as the division director or head of school. Perhaps there needs to be a conversation about whether or not there is a need to hire an additional college counselor. In that scenario, several people may be involved in that conversation, and you will take the consensus approach. In each case, explain the why behind the decision making model. This approach can also be used when talking at home about where to go for dinner on Friday night. Perhaps we will have a consensus because we have the time to discuss it and go back and forth. We may be in a time crunch as we need to be somewhere after, so a top down decision is made. These seem like simple decisions, but letting your family know how you are making decisions goes a long way in developing and building a relationship.

SHARE YOUR MISTAKES BEFORE TALKING ABOUT SOMEONE ELSE'S: We all are aware of our own mistakes, regardless of whether we want to admit them or not. Some of us are better at acknowledging and sharing their mistakes than others. People on your team respect honesty, transparency and vulnerability. This last one has recently taken root in the realm of leadership, and it is important to showcase it to your team. The stereotypical leader who never shows pain or discomfort, who is always willing to arrive early and stay late, no matter how tired they are, is no longer idolized or praised. Leaders need to model risk-taking and failure so their team can follow. Vulnerability is also "a powerful tool in emotionally intelligent managers," Harvey Deutschendorf, an emotional intelligence expert, says in an article in Fast Company. That's because vulnerability is closely tied to trust, and trust is the keystone of strong (resilient) relationships. If it is okay for the leader to make a mistake, that allows others to feel comfortable making them too. It is important we do not seek to make mistakes. Take calculated risks as opposed to ill-advised gambles. This is like Jim Collins' shooting bullets instead of cannon balls. Too many costly mistakes or too large of a mistake and the organization can take a big hit. In the end, we are all accountable and need to share that across all levels by owning our mistakes and being vulnerable.

GIVE PRAISE AND SHOW APPRECIATION: I grew up in a time and in a household where you did what was asked, and it didn't matter how you felt about the task. All that mattered was whether you did or did not complete the task. Praise was not offered much, which was a by-product of the times, yet it did not keep me from performing well in school or on the athletic field. This stayed with me as I began a career in education that included coaching. In the years that have passed, as a leader of adults, I have realized that praise and appreciation are needed and often deserved. This is also true for our students in schools. If I want our faculty and coaches to offer praise, I need to model it. People who are committed to the organization, the task and each other deserve to be acknowledged for the productive and positive contributions they make.

This is not to say everyone is deserving of praise and appreciation for meeting all tasks. We also should not give false praise as that will lead to poor results in the long run. We need standards in our lives and organizations in order to be successful. Meeting these standards such as arriving to work on time or fulfilling a duty is not worthy of praise on a daily basis. If arriving on time also included morning extra help sessions with a student who came in early to meet with a teacher, I believe that is worthy of acknowledgement. This may look different at home with children but is arguably more important there. Children need to know that the effort, work or time they are contributing at home is important and appreciated. They need to build a skill set around kindness and contributing to the greater good. Children should be praised when they take actions in these areas. Children who grow up receiving praise and appreciation will provide it to others along their journey, and that is a legacy we should all strive for as parents because it will help create a kinder, more respectful world. Simply acknowledging the completion of a task such as taking out the trash or emptying the dishwasher and offering thanks will likely ensure the task is completed again. This combination of praise and encouragement helps forge a sense of belonging and responsibility.

STAY ENGAGED AND PROVIDE ENCOURAGEMENT: We want to be wary of micromanaging or checking in too often with our teams. That said, we should not just hand off a task and wait until the deadline to see how it is going. Check in on your team, and provide encouragement to continue with the task. Ask questions:

- Are you where you want to be with the project?
- What has gone well and can you replicate it?
- What unexpected obstacles are you facing?
- How can I help?

If each question comes from a place of curiosity, you will be pleasantly surprised at the response of your team. If the questions are perceived as oversight, the response will likely be different. To be clear, the responsibility for the response falls on you as the leader. People can see through false sincerity. Asking questions because you feel like you have to or to manipulate the team will not work. You have to care about the individuals doing the work as well as the work being done. Modeling this as a school leader is vitally important as it is the same behavior you want your faculty to demonstrate in the classroom with their students. This transfers easily to the home with children as well. This is not being nosy or overbearing, but rather it is about being present in their lives. Your children are not always going to receive the encouragement they need or are seeking outside of your home, so it is important they hear it. This is not to create an unrealistic environment but to acknowledge they can and will go farther if they commit to the work

ALWAYS HAVE A PLAN AND BE WILLING TO CHANGE IT AS NECESSARY: As former president Dwight Eisenhower stated, "Plans are useless, but planning is indispensable." We cannot go into any day, week, month, or semester without a plan. Every meeting you have should include a plan, no matter how small. Your direct report may not get to meet with you very often, and they deserve your full attention during that time. This requires planning on your part: set aside a specific amount of time, have an agenda with questions or ask them to provide the agenda if they requested the meeting; listen, and be present. Create a plan for following up. Larger plans may require benchmarks and metrics as you move towards a strategic plan or vision. This is usually long term and may require reflections along the way to see if the plan is still working. If not, change it, and explain why it is being changed. Perhaps there is something out of our control in the market or the economy. We cannot ignore external factors and just continue on our way. We do not have to throw the plan out and start over, but we do have to be willing to adjust and adapt as necessary. We may need to rethink our strategy or approach. In Adam Grant's book, *Think Again: The Power of Knowing What You Don't Know*, he invites his readers to "…let go of knowledge and opinions that are no longer serving you well and to anchor your sense of self in flexibility rather than consistency."

USE THE 20–MILE MARCH APPROACH: In *Great by Choice: Uncertainty, Chaos, and Luck-Why Some Thrive Despite Them All*, Jim Collins shares a story about the race to the South Pole. The winning team, led by Roald Amundsen, focused on an approach that required discipline and allowed for minor changes, but he did not allow external factors to completely disrupt his plan. He committed to covering 20 miles each day, whatever the weather conditions. This meant having the discipline on the best days to stop and break for camp when the team felt they could march on, and it also meant getting up in the morning on the bitterest of days. With this in mind, there were some days when they only went 15 miles or 17 miles because the conditions were so harsh. He made adjustments as needed but maintained the discipline of pushing forward each day. Conversely, his counterpart, Robert Falcon Scott, who was also racing to the South Pole, took a different approach. His team would push as hard as possible on the great days covering some 40-60 miles but would hunker down in tents and stay put on the harshest of days. Unfortunately, Scott's entire team perished 10 miles from the destination and well after Amundsen's team had already reached the South Pole. It is imperative that you are consistent in your pursuit, and recognize that unfavorable days may outnumber the favorable days. A disciplined approach will see you through to the end. There are many demands on the schedule of a school leader, and it can be difficult to meet all of them on a daily basis. You may want to schedule a specific number of classroom visits per day or week instead of setting a goal to visit every class by a certain date. By scheduling your visits and keeping them on your calendar, you are more likely to meet this goal. I have been doing this for several years now and label the time as my walkabouts. My administrative assistant knows that these times are important and should not be cut for meetings unless it is absolutely necessary.

BE ASSERTIVE – CHOOSING NOT TO ACT IS STILL A DECISION: Choices present themselves on a daily basis, and we need to make decisions. It is important to know that choosing to wait or stall is still a decision. You have to acknowledge that, and let your team know if that is what you are doing. It keeps them from being in the dark and wondering why you have not reached out or provided an update. If possible, include an explanation for your thought process. Waiting does not make the problem go away. Too often, we delay making a difficult decision even though we know what to do because it is difficult, and we want to avoid it. This only makes the decision more challenging. Think about a time when you needed to provide critical feedback to a colleague or subordinate. Each day that goes by, you get further from the incident that required the feedback. In most cases, the individual will have moved on and will not fully understand why you are concerned or giving the feedback. Communicating to your team on a regular basis is a must. Choosing not to do so is a decision that can have negative consequences for you and the organization. I can think of situations as a leader in a school when I did not directly address a concern in the moment and let it go. This can create a new standard in the mind of the individual, and they may think their actions were appropriate. The longer you wait, the harder the conversation becomes.

DESIGN AND IMPLEMENTATION IS AN ITERATIVE PROCESS: In many cases there is no immediate solution to the challenges we are facing. You often need time to identify the problem and develop solutions with your team. In this work, you will not always be ready to give a final answer. In the meantime, you can take steps in the direction you believe to be correct. As you move towards the solution, consider these questions: Where are we? What have we accomplished?

The answers will let you know if the team is still on the right path. On the surface, this may appear to be less efficient than moving straight to the perceived answer, yet it saves time in the long run, especially if you were wrong. The environment and climate around you can change in a moment's notice, and you have to be prepared for that. If you rush into the solution and do not stop to evaluate, it is possible you will end up straying from the path and likely fail to reach the target. This is how lesson planning can go for teachers. The plan appears great before the bell rings and students are in front of you. If it does not strike the right chord with the students or they are failing to understand the objectives, make a change. As long as you keep the objectives in mind, iterating in the moment and staying on the path makes sense. While you should be confident in your plans, you should never hold onto them so tightly that you cannot change them when needed.

BE WARY OF PLANNING FALLACY: We often fail to take into account how long it will take to complete a task or the mission. We are all guilty of this. Even knowing it exists does not mean we are able to avoid it. We can mitigate it by planning our day accordingly. The first step is to identify your most important task (MIT) for the day. There should never be more than three. While these tasks do not have to happen first thing, they do have to happen during the day. By writing down and identifying them, you are sure to complete your tasks and not let one that runs longer than anticipated (planning fallacy) keep you from completing them all. The second step is to take care of the most challenging task first thing in the morning. Too often, we put it off until later, then we do not get to it. Before we know it, the task keeps showing up day after day on our to-do list, and with each day that goes by, it becomes more difficult to complete. The planning fallacy strikes all of us, but we can take steps to mitigate it. At the end of each week, I review my calendar, then schedule blocks of time for the following week to ensure I can meet deadlines and complete tasks. I consider upcoming events, responsibilities or tasks that I will need to complete and build in time to accomplish them. I also talk with my administrative assistant about which time blocks cannot be rescheduled or reshuffled and which can, in the event something unexpected happens. I also take the time to look a month out to see where I need to begin planning for future events on campus.

KNOW YOUR PEOPLE AND YOUR TEAM: Team success in any school or organization is built on trust. Trust comes from building relationships, and strong relationships come from consistent, positive interactions. People have to know that you care for them, and that is not possible without frequent conversations and interactions. As Theodore Roosevelt stated, "People don't care how much you know until they know how much you care." It also requires a genuine curiosity on the part of the leader. You should know all of your direct reports both personally and professionally. You should be aware of their professional goals as well as their personal situation. Take an interest in their growth and development within the organization. Ask questions and listen carefully to their responses.

- What do you want to accomplish while you are in this organization?
- What is your long term plan for your role?
- How can I help you achieve it?

Be sure to ask about family and hobbies or extracurricular activities. Everyone wants to feel a sense of belonging, and this occurs when we make connections through conversation and relationship building.

EVERYONE SHOULD BE TREATED FAIRLY – FAIR DOES NOT ALWAYS MEAN EQUAL: This is one of the hardest lessons to learn and even harder to teach. There is an inherent belief by many that fair means equal, which it does not. Everyone has different needs in order to be on the same playing field. This does not mean you or someone else should be given an advantage over the other person. Identify the situation, and make a decision that is fair to all parties. One example in education has to do with extended time on assessments. It takes some students more time to read or process material than another. Two students may have the same knowledge and expertise, but because it takes one longer to express it, giving them the same time limit is not fair. If you are not grading for speed, the time required to complete the assessment is not important. It is equal if you give everyone as much time as they want to complete the task, but, once again, not fair. There may be tasks or assignments that do require deadlines and timeliness. This is not to say you cannot impose those deadlines, but be clear on why they exist and why they need to be met. In your household, all of your children are not treated the same, especially when you have a gap in years. Every parent has heard, "Why does she get to stay up later than me?" The reality is that different aged children have different sleep requirements. That is not always easy to explain to a child, but the sooner they learn that fair is not equal, the better off they will be. This was a challenge for me in my early years as a head lacrosse coach. I thought all of my players should be treated exactly the same, regardless of ability, personality, or anything else. I did not take the time to learn enough about each player to know how they would respond to feedback or to my style as a coach. It was not until much later that I realized some of my players responded to one-on-one conversations much better than public conversations.

BUILD AND MAINTAIN A STRONG CULTURE: Your culture is the rock that stands up to the pounding waves. If you do not pay attention, it gets worn down and washed away. There are challenges and opportunities facing you and your organization every day. The ability to respond and move forward is tied to culture. Everyone in the organization needs to know what it means to work and exist within the framework of your company's culture. People feel it and see it every day. They point to it when things go well and, equally, when things do not go well. You might hear someone say, "Well, what did you expect? That is the culture here." This can be said in a sarcastic manner by someone who dreads coming to work every day, or it can be said proudly by the person who feels fortunate to show up and work for your organization. Refer to the culture often, and help others see how it exists in day-to-day operations. Get feedback on your culture, and ask people to share why it is important. It has to be maintained. Every time we allow a sub-standard email to go out, excuse an inappropriate comment or run a meeting poorly, we are setting a new standard. That impacts culture because people see it and know it is not right, but they do not address it. This can quickly spiral downward, and the culture becomes nothing more than a punchline. It has to be lived daily. Remember that culture is hard to establish, harder to change, and hardest to maintain. You have to work at maintaining it as a leader and get the support from your team to help.

DECISIONS MUST BE SUPPORTED ACROSS THE BOARD, TOP-DOWN: Similar to support for the culture, there needs to be clear support for all decisions. This does not mean you should surround yourself with yes men who do not challenge ideas. Diverse thought creates space for an exchange of ideas. The back and forth discussion often leads to the best outcome possible in the decision making process but is made challenging if people do not see value in this exchange. A team member who believes they always have the best idea can be toxic. As a leader, it is crucial that you establish a culture that is open to all ideas and model acceptance of all ideas. The final decision that comes out of the room needs to be supported, otherwise there will be cracks in the implementation because not everyone sees the benefit or the need to do it correctly. Leaders need to openly seek conversation, discussion and even disagreements. They also need to have conversations about supporting the decision outside of the room, with no concession to personal opinion. Pat Lencioni shares a few points about the importance of this in his book *Five Dysfunctions of a Team: A Leadership Fable*. At the end of your meeting, write the decision on the board and make sure everyone understands it. If there needs to be more discussion, then have it. Next, he discusses the importance of "cascading communication." Once the decision is made, your team members have 24 hours to share the information with their direct reports and it needs to happen in person so questions can be addressed in the moment. In the event you hear a team member is not delivering the information or is not supporting the decisions, there needs to be a one-on-one conversation with the person who broke rank to understand why. This is not a time to accuse the individual or to fire them but rather to understand why they made the choice, to explain the importance of supporting team decisions and how to move forward. If it happens again, the next conversation may have to involve a sterner approach that includes a warning about the potential for losing their job.

EVERYONE ON THE TEAM IS IMPORTANT – TELL THEM: We hear this growing up in team sports, youth groups, or dance troupes. The problem is that the people saying it do not always model it. The players with less talent near the end of the roster get less attention and less feedback than the more talented players. The students with greater ability tend to get more attention in and out of the classroom, sometimes even at home. The reality is that you cannot have a basketball team with only four players. For that matter, to be a good team, it helps to have 10 so you can scrimmage and provide game-like experiences. Player #10 on the depth chart needs to be seen and recognized by the coach. They need to know that they are important to the team's overall success, even if they do not step on the court in a game, because the winning result comes from the work beforehand – practicing. A school community cannot run without the people preparing lunches every day or fixing the broken window or driving the bus. The fact of the matter is, the school cannot run effectively and efficiently without everyone on the team pulling in the same direction. Reach out to these individuals and let them know how important they are to the success of the school and how much you appreciate the work they do. Use their names when saying thank you. This act of knowing the names of all of your employees is the first and, potentially, most important step in acknowledging their value to the team.

CLEARLY DEFINE ROLES AND RESPONSIBILITIES: Each time a new employee joins the team, take the opportunity to clearly define roles and responsibilities. That is key for the new staff member and also an important reminder to current team members. There may be overlap of duties and this is where the leader needs to give clear guidance and direction. There may be equal colleagues collaborating on a project, and you may give them the autonomy to divide up the work. However, you may also want to have some clear directives outlined in the task about individual responsibilities. This leaves no room for questioning or finger pointing at the end. This is also helpful in a household with children as we work to develop a sense of purpose and commitment to a larger group. If it is everyone's responsibility to empty the dishwasher or feed the dog, too often it does not happen and falls to the parent. By defining roles and responsibilities for your children, it gives them a sense of belonging and starts them on the path of accountability and collaboration.

IDENTIFY PROBLEMS EARLY ON AND ADDRESS THEM: As a leader, you are responsible for identifying the road blocks within your team and organization. You have to seek out the problems before they grow and negatively impact results. Identifying the problems is not the difficult part; all you have to do is look around and you can find a problem. The difficult part is addressing the problem. When doing so, you have to dig to find the root of the problem, and it is rarely what you first suspect. Once there, you can begin to work towards resolution by asking questions and seeking clarity. In some instances, you will not actually be the one solving the problem but asking the questions that lead to the solution. The more conversations you have and questions you ask, the fewer problems you will have within the organization. In a staff meeting, one of your faculty members may make a questionable comment. The initial response may be to address the comment publicly or privately. Unless it is egregious, it should not be done publicly. If you do have to address it publicly, the person should not be humiliated or made to feel less about themselves. A simple response can be, "Thank you, but now is not that time for that discussion" or "Thank you, we can discuss that at a later date while we keep our focus on the current task." Once you have the private conversation, the first question should not be "Why did you say that?" or worse yet, "What were you thinking?" Instead, the better response could be, "I would like to better understand the comment you made in our meeting. Can you clarify it for me?" You want to show compassion for the work they do. Depending on your relationship, you may also ask about family or personal life. There is something going on that led to the action of the inappropriate comment, and that should be the direction you take the conversation. Once you find the root, you can work with the individual on how to move forward.

SET STANDARDS AND LIVE BY THEM – UNDERSTAND THE DIFFERENCE BETWEEN STANDARDS AND GOALS:

Standards are the expectations we lay out for ourselves and our team every day. For example, we arrive at work on time, we respond to colleagues within 24 hours, and we treat everyone on the team with respect. Goals are benchmarks we hope to reach and often include action items to help us get there. If set correctly, we may not always reach them. It is okay to not reach a goal as long as we understand what happened and why we did not reach it. We have the ability to reset the goal and go after it again. There may have been circumstances beyond your control that intervened, or you may have set the bar too high in a particular "stretch" goal (high-effort, high-risk goal). This is not true of standards, and it is not acceptable for you or your team members to fail to meet standards. Those are non-negotiable. Whenever possible, you should include your team in developing and identifying the standards. This will lead to greater buy-in and also result in team members holding each other accountable. Another way to look at standards can be norms. Prior to the start of the year, you may gather with your leadership team and discuss the importance of meeting norms. As a group, you discuss various norms, perhaps even the ones used previously, and identify norms for the current year. Each school year brings its own unique challenges and opportunities, therefore, you should work with the team every year on setting norms. This was not always my practice as a school leader. I was a believer that norms should not change as they represented our culture and my values as a leader. I have come to realize that my approach failed to take into account the views or perspectives of others. This is especially important when you add a new member to your leadership team or faculty.

RECOGNIZE WHEN YOU CHOOSE TO RATIONALIZE OR CHANGE A STANDARD: Our standards should not be compromised, and circumstances should not dictate our decision making. This is a general rule that you and your team should maintain. That said, there may be times that we need to evaluate a standard because of the specific scenario. In this particular case, be clear on what you are doing and why you are doing it. You may have a strong teacher who is often late to work. If you are choosing to look the other way because of their work in the classroom, you are rationalizing their lack of adherence to the rule and must take ownership of that decision. This can have a negative effect on team morale and have people questioning the standard. In another scenario, it may be time to evaluate the school's dress code based on current societal and cultural norms.

Some of our standards and policies may no longer be relevant, but we choose to keep them because we have always had them. Once you recognize this outdated thinking and begin the process of making a change, it is important to include your leadership team in the conversation as well as your students and families. If you make changes, explain to the entire organization how and why the changes were made.

HIRE THE RIGHT PEOPLE WITH ALIGNMENT IN MIND: Every team and every organization thrives based on culture. Good people leave organizations if the culture is not strong or if they see colleagues allowed to remain at the school even though their values contradict the school's values or if they are not doing the same work as their colleagues. Schools, just like other organizations, need to look at competencies when hiring and move beyond the specific demands of the job. Most tasks and responsibilities can be learned, especially if the person is a good match for the organization and has a desire to learn. A person can bring all of the knowledge and expertise, but if they lack the value based competencies you want, they will negatively impact culture. As a leader, you are responsible for the culture. When hiring, you should never lower the bar, but rather wait and keep looking. This is much easier said than done. There are times when circumstances may impact hiring decisions because we cannot survive long term with a hole in the organization. Set a deadline by which you can survive without a hire, and if you feel it is absolutely necessary to make a hire, put them on an interim basis or probationary status. You do not have to call it that, but provide a quarterly or six-month review at which point the new employee knows that their employment will be extended, or they will be relieved of the position. This can be especially difficult when looking to hire a teacher and the summer days are passing quickly. Ultimately, you may need to choose the best candidate from a shallow pool. Identify what competencies are non-negotiable and seek the candidate who matches them. Be sure to place them with a strong mentor, and have a support plan in place prior to the start of the year.

BE CAREFUL HOW YOU USE BLAME OR CREDIT AND CONSIDER USING ACCURATE OR INACCURATE: In a leadership role, people are always paying attention to what you say and what you do. If you look to blame your team or employees regularly, people won't bring you bad news and will avoid you. Colin Powell pointed out the issue with this when he said, "The day soldiers stop bringing you their problems is the day you have stopped leading them. They have either lost confidence that you can help or concluded you do not care." Either way, the outcome is you not having all of the information you need to make good decisions in the best interest of the company or organization. Likewise, we need to be mindful of who we are giving credit to and how we deliver it. If it was truly a team effort, state that and name each individual. Giving credit to only the team leader can create animosity. Beyond blame and credit, the use of the phrases accurate and inaccurate helps to provide a more objective view point. That was an inaccurate prediction by the team, as opposed to the team was wrong to assume we would see growth in our admission cycle for the 9th grade. Objectivity helps eliminate a sense of fair/unfair or even a belief the boss has a favorite staff member.

HEALTHY CONFLICT IS GOOD: While we frequently see displays of conflict on social media and in the news, we tend to avoid conflict in the workplace. We often seek ways to side step difficult conversations as we worry about the impact it will have on interoffice politics. Perhaps this is, in part, due to the poor modeling that is all around us. You turn on the news and you see political parties yelling over each other. Looking for a break, you turn to sports, only to hear anchors or talk show hosts doing the same, exact thing. These are often baseless and pointless arguments in which no one is listening to the other person. That is not healthy conflict. In order to have healthy conflict, everyone has to agree to listen to each other and to accept the views of others even if they do not agree. We should hold our thoughts and opinions lightly so as not to get bogged down into political warfare. It has been said the room is the smartest person in the conversation. Essentially, the collective wisdom of the group produces the greatest insight instead of the loudest individual. When we engage in healthy conflict and dialogue, we get diverse thought that leads to better outcomes. Within your leadership team, there should be a healthy balance of advocacy and inquiry. Individuals should advocate for their ideas or suggestions, and they should also be curious about those of their teammates. We should inquire how a decision or suggestion was reached. When we get curious and ask questions, we learn more. If we simply talk and do not listen, we are not able to learn and, instead, cling to our own beliefs.

ENSURE MEANINGFUL RELATIONSHIPS EXIST IN YOUR ORGANIZATION TO SUPPORT MEANINGFUL WORK: Everyone needs to feel a sense of belonging to the organization and feel welcome. If individuals are left to feel like interchangeable cogs, the relationships won't exist as they need to in order to allow for meaningful work. When you are committed to each other and the organization, you want to do your best. You recognize the importance of your role and do not want to disappoint those around you. You develop those relationships by checking in with your team and having conversations about topics other than work. You know about their family, their goals, their purpose. This requires effort on the part of the leader; be intentional about the work. Your role as a team leader involves a great deal of time and attention. Many of your days are filled with meetings, phone calls, and appointments. Model the importance of developing meaningful relationships by building connections into your calendar. Set specific times of day, every day, to engage with co-workers. If you are not intentional in setting a schedule, you will not follow through.

BE HONEST AND TRANSPARENT WITH YOUR TEAM: When people do not have all of the answers, they often make up answers, no matter how wrong they might be. When issues arise and you get to the root cause, talk to the team. If someone has to be let go, explain why the decision was made. If there is a new mandate from the Board of Directors, talk to the team about the why and the how behind the decision. If you are unsure of what to say or how to explain something, you can say that as well. Provide the information that you have and share what you can. That said, there will be times you have to keep information confidential, and you can state that in an appropriate and healthy manner. It must be done correctly so the team does not feel like you are deliberately keeping them in the dark or misleading them. For example, a colleague has a leave of absence or perhaps resigned due to a health crisis in their family. You simply inform the team that the person made a difficult decision to resign and you cannot share all of the details, but that individual wants you to know how much they enjoyed working with you and in the organization. They will miss the team and plan to stay in touch. People will believe you and respect the need for confidentiality if you are consistently honest and transparent with them. This was the case for many individuals in education during the pandemic. Not every teacher was comfortable returning to the classroom and had to make personal decisions. It is not your right to share their information, but it is right to keep your team informed.

COMMUNICATE OFTEN AND EFFECTIVELY: When it comes to communication, each day you should ask yourself three questions:

- What do I know?
- Who else needs to know it?
- Have I told them?

Leaders can take information for granted because it is always coming at them from all directions. We sometimes fail to realize that individuals in the organization do not have access to all of the same information. It is your job to deliver it and do so effectively. This means using multiple modalities: verbal, written, and presentation (when appropriate). The idea of using a need-to-know approach is outdated and alienates your team. This is especially true when you as the leader are engaged in conversations that your team is not a part of during a given day or week. Your role is to bring information back so they can help you execute the plan. It gives them insight into the decisions being made and helps them support the overall vision and mission. The more frequently you can remind yourself to do this, the greater trust will exist across the organization.

BE CLEAR WITH EXPECTATIONS: When tasks are not completed to the liking of the leader, it is often the leaders fault. While there are some individuals who believe it is always the leader's fault, I will not take it that far. In order to understand your role in the substandard performance, you need to reflect on your communication with the team. Ask yourself the following questions:

- Did I clearly outline the expectations?
- Was I explicit with what I wanted done and how?
- If you were not clear, you must be comfortable letting your team make those decisions, and you have to accept the outcome.

There is a fine line with expectations as you can easily become a micromanager. If there is an upset parent and you ask a department chair to have a conversation with the parent but provide no other guidance, the outcome is the outcome. The chair did what they thought was best. If that is not enough for you, go back to the request you made. You were not overly detailed or clear. If you wanted the chair to resolve the issue, then you should have said that. A great way to avoid micromanaging is to borrow a phrase from Brené Brown: "Paint it done for me." Now when you say, "I need you to talk to a parent who is frustrated with your grading philosophy," you follow it up with, "after you hang up the phone, 'paint it done for me.'" In other words, share your plan with me.

LOOK FOR PATTERNS – BOTH POSITIVE AND NEGATIVE:

Everyone has positive and negative experiences during their day. As a leader, identify patterns within your daily interactions and also within your organization. Consider looking for specific times of the day or interactions with specific individuals (colleagues, students, parents) that create these patterns. Again, be open to looking for both types of interactions. There is a danger in looking only for positive interactions as you may fail to see the impact of negative interactions on the team. Likewise, if your team only hears about the negative, they begin to question whether your culture has any level of positivity. There is a balance you should seek as the leader.

The next step is determining how to create or accentuate positive experiences and limit the negative experiences. You will not be able to eliminate all negative experiences, but you can mitigate them if you are able to see the pattern. More importantly, leaders need to find ways to create more positive experiences in the day-to-day interactions of your team. Is it something tangible like the type of coffee in the workroom or catered Friday lunches? Is it relaxed dress days? You have to know your team to see where you can build the positive experiences and you have to understand the team culture. Sticky note compliments or thank-yous on doors or people's desks can go a long way. Share good news with the team as often as possible such as weddings or births. In strong organizations, people care about their co-workers or teammates and enjoy sharing in this type of news. You have to set the tone as the leader and build a positive culture.

MANAGING IS IMPORTANT – KNOWING WHEN YOU HAVE TO MICROMANAGE IS MORE IMPORTANT: All leaders are managers, but not all managers are leaders. It takes focused effort and constant learning to serve as a leader. In working with your team, it is important that you are aware of the work that is happening and that you get updates on the work. This can be done through a variety of ways. You will get the most buy-in through delegation and by giving autonomy to your team. Letting the team know about your interest in updates is not about micromanaging, but rather it is about having the knowledge to share with other teams, the Board of Directors or your boss. It also lets you see if there is a need to step in and micromanage. If there is a looming deadline and you are not seeing the progress that is needed, you may have to inquire about the team's ability to meet the deadline and perhaps even offer some suggestions. Depending on what happens next, you may need to take a more direct approach in which you set incremental deadlines that need to be met along the way. This is micromanaging, at this point, and you will not be able to do this with all of your direct reports over the long haul. As a leader, you have too much to do. After this deadline comes and goes, there needs to be a debrief or post project analysis. The challenges and roadblocks need to be discussed as well as expectations moving forward and potential consequences for failing to meet those expectations.

It is important to recognize that micromanaging is not a long-term solution. Be aware of when it is necessary, and be firm on how long you will implement it. You also want to explain to the team how you reached this point and the steps everyone needs to take to ensure it is not required again.

SEEK AND GIVE FEEDBACK CONSISTENTLY: Everyone wants to know when they are doing well and likes to receive praise. On the other hand, not everyone wants to know where they need to improve. If you are hiring right and making good personnel decisions, the people on your team want to learn, grow and improve. This can only happen with coaching and feedback. In order to create a culture that seeks feedback, you have to model this approach. Take the first step, and seek feedback from others. This will require pushing your team for information because it will, most likely, start out shallow and surface level. Your direct reports are likely to be nervous to give feedback to you, regardless of how accepting of the information you promise to be or how reassuring you are. In order to effectively give and receive feedback, there has to be trust in the working relationship and a certain level of psychological safety. When you receive the feedback, ask clarifying questions, and thank the person for sharing it with you. You should reflect on the feedback, and take 24-48 hours to determine how you can implement this. By making a plan in the moment, you are not giving enough thought to the feedback, and if it extends much beyond 48 hours, it appears you are not prioritizing the feedback. Share out your reflection and steps with the individual who provided the feedback. If appropriate, you can share this with more team members as a way to show them that you are open to feedback and will implement it when applicable. As you model this and seek feedback frequently, you will soon see a shift in culture. Team members will openly share feedback with one another, and this will raise the level of everyone's work and contributions to the team. You can do this in your weekly or bi-weekly check-in meetings when you ask your subordinates for feedback. You can also put out anonymous surveys for feedback, then share the results for everyone to see. You can schedule a meeting with your boss and ask directly for feedback.

HOLD YOURSELF AND OTHERS ACCOUNTABLE: Self-imposed discipline is the best form of discipline and one that you should strive to have in your organization. As the leader you can set this example and show others how to do it. Let your team know when you fall short on a goal or do not meet a standard. Explain what happened. Do not make an excuse and try to rationalize it; just state what happened and how you plan to address it. Let others see that you are human and fallible. When it comes time to hold others accountable, they will know that you are accountable as well because of this transparency and modeling. Ideally, they too will begin to develop self-imposed discipline and make better choices going forward that will help the team and themselves.

ALLOW OTHERS TO HOLD YOU ACCOUNTABLE: It is important that you also let others hold you accountable and not just rely on your own ability to do so. We have our own implicit biases and blind spots that prevent us from seeing how our words or actions fully impact our team. For example, I know if I am late for a meeting, it impacts the people waiting for me. Conversely, I may not realize that a comment I make in a meeting may leave some members of the team questioning my support for them or my level of empathy. This is tied directly to seeking feedback from others. Let people bring you information, and listen to them when it comes time for feedback and accountability.

A recent example of this is how different individuals felt about working during the pandemic starting in the spring of 2020. Some leaders may not have been hesitant at all and forged ahead without seeking feedback from those with fears and concerns. If we minimalize their comments in an effort to persuade them to come to work, we show a lack of empathy and negatively impact our relationship. I know I was guilty of this at times and needed to hear directly from people about how my comments impacted those individuals. I apologized to them in one-on-one conversations and also in front of our team.

BUILD AROUND GOALS NOT TASKS: Whether or not you have long-term or short-term goals, your focus should be on the areas that will help you reach those goals. If your life is run by your to-do list and your task list, you likely will not reach your goals. Tasks give us short term rewards and instant gratification - everyone loves to cross off an item on their to-do list as it provides us with a sense of accomplishment. That said, it is likely, many of the items on that list are not directly tied to your goals. Make your goals visible and accessible to you daily so that you can ensure at least a portion of your day includes work related to these goals. For example, a check-list item may be to visit classrooms today. A goal oriented item, may be to build positive relationships with faculty by checking in frequently and communicating. I could visit a teacher's classroom, but if

I do not follow up in a timely manner or have a check-in with them, I failed in my goal and relationship building. I did check off the to-do list item because I got into the classroom, but nothing of merit was accomplished. Checking off items on your to-do list may feel good in the moment, but at the end of the year, you are left with sheets of paper that have tasks crossed out and you find yourself in the same exact place.

LOOK OUT AND UP INSTEAD OF IN AND DOWN: Leaders need to be able to see around corners and into the future to prepare their school for what lies ahead. This is not possible when we are looking in and down. This is associated with ineffective leadership and can manifest in a few ways. We could be looking at all of the information in front of us and simply never look up to see what else is available to us or what else is happening. We can become so focused on trying to make a decision that we end up in a situation known as paralysis by analysis. We also fail to look to others for help or suggestions when we are looking in and down. We miss out on the chance to get feedback and collect information from our team. By looking out and up we can see the entire landscape in front of us, we are able to observe any changes, and our colleagues can see us looking for opportunities. There is also a level of confidence that comes just from the actual posture of looking out and up. It is important to schedule time for introspection and looking within, but that is not the case when decisions need to be made. Many school leaders were faced with the difficult decision about whether or not to have in-person learning during the 2020-2021 school year. There was an overload of information and plenty of people with opinions on what to do. In order to make effective decisions about the steps to take, school leaders had to look into the future. They had to consider various contingencies and get feedback on those contingencies from colleagues and team members. A leader who simply looked inward and was unsure of what steps to take failed their team.

DETACH FROM THE MOMENT: Leaders need to respond, not react. That happens more consistently if you are able to detach. Step back from the events unfolding and look at what is happening around you. In some cases, it is literally moving back from the table in the boardroom, in others it is leaving the room or the environment all together. We may not always be able to physically detach, therefore we have to practice mentally detaching. Take a deep breath, and start to observe what is happening around you, notice how people are talking to each other, what is being said, who is doing the talking. Listen and observe. Practice the OODA Loop: observe, orient, decide, act (initially referenced in chapter 2). To be clear, the last part may include more observation, act does not have to include physically moving or doing anything; remember, inaction is still a decision and, in fact, a different type of action.

> *"Leadership is about empathy. It is about having the ability to relate to and connect with people for the purpose of inspiring and empowering their lives."*
> *– Oprah Winfrey*

The principles in this chapter are to serve as guidelines for you as a school leader. You may not follow each one every day, but they should be at the core of the work you are doing. Your faculty and direct reports are in need of your support and leadership. You are the model for all of them, and they are always aware of your words and actions. A humble leader seeks input from those around them and recognizes individuals who contribute to the greater good of the team. This is what you want to see from your teachers and coaches in the community, so model it often. When making decisions, engage your stakeholders and be open to the ideas of others. Think and rethink about the process as well as the outcome. In Adam Grant's book, *Think Again: The Power of Knowing What You Don't Know*, he reminds us,

> Thinking again can help you generate new solutions to old problems and revisit old solutions to new problems. It's a path to learning more from the people around you and living with fewer regrets. A hallmark of wisdom is knowing when it's time to abandon some of your most treasured tools.

You can build a strong culture with this mindset and with consistent communication to your team. Frequent and transparent communication creates strong and trusting relationships, which are at the core of teaching. Be sure to hold yourself and others accountable for meeting the standards and striving toward goals.

EXAMPLE:

PRINCIPLE: Detaching and utilizing the OODA Loop

WHAT I DID BEFORE: In weekly meetings with my team, we often discussed students we were concerned about. Team members brought students to the table for the discussion. I would ask for feedback, suggestions and thoughts. I often had my own ideas about how we could help the student. As the conversation continued, my personal beliefs and feelings could inadvertently shift from task conflict to a personal conflict. Task conflict is healthy and often leads to better decision making in the end. Personal conflict created roadblocks. If I held onto my ideas too strongly, the solution was harder to reach, and one of the team members often left frustrated or disgruntled and did not like the solution.

WHAT I WANT TO DO DIFFERENTLY: I want to recognize when the task conflict is shifting to a personal conflict. At that point, I want to detach and look at the conflict objectively. I want to ask others to also participate in this approach and share the idea of the OODA Loop so we can ensure our focus remains on finding a solution to the task.

HOW WILL I ACCOMPLISH THIS:

- I will introduce the idea of task conflict versus personal conflict and ask the team to share experiences with this.
- I will introduce the OODA Loop and ask team members to reflect on a time where this would have helped in a personal or professional conversation.

- I will be intentional and state when we are utilizing the OODA Loop and detaching from the conflict for a moment so we can pause and reflect.
- I will ask team members to utilize this approach in meetings they lead and ask them to share their experience at future meetings.

QUESTIONS TO CONSIDER:

- Are you the type of leader that you would follow? Why or why not?
- Are you humble in your interactions?
- What are your strengths as a leader?
- Where would you like to improve as a leader?
- Is your communication style clear, effective and timely?
- Are you looking out and up consistently to see what is coming?

CHAPTER 4
LEADERSHIP STRATEGIES

Every one of us is a leader in some capacity in our life. At the very least, we are leading ourselves every day and need to make decisions that support our growth and ability. You might also be a leader in your household or at work. Many of the strategies and behaviors required for good leadership are the result of developing good habits and healthy relationships with those around you. It also requires reflection and a commitment to growth.

SUPPORTING NEW LEADERS: Set the bar high and model leadership behaviors for new leaders to emulate. As Marshall Goldsmith said, "What got you here, won't get you there." Every new leader was successful in their previous role, which is why they moved into this new role. That said, some of their strengths and the reasons they were promoted will not be enough to help them be a successful leader. As the person who hired or appointed them, it is your job to provide them with guidance, support and coaching. It will also require modeling as this individual is going to be watching and listening to you on a daily basis. I know I did not receive enough of this when I stepped into my current role. I also bear responsibility in that I did not actively seek it out. If you have new leaders working for you or you are a new leader yourself, you must be intentional in your growth.

BE HUMBLE: No one has all of the answers, no matter how much experience they have in life. You may have had experiences that provide you with more insight and knowledge, but how you present these experiences and go about learning more is equally as important. There is also a distinct possibility that a member of your team knows something you do not. Ask questions of that person; ask questions of everyone on your team, and seek feedback. When you share a plan you developed, ask others for input and suggestions. To go one step further, ask others to develop the plan. Last, humility is not a "sometimes" behavior, either you bring humility to all of your work and interactions or you do not. Your team can see through it when you occasionally ask questions or occasionally apologize. You can be seen as manipulative and that is not a path you want to go down as a leader.

ASK GOOD QUESTIONS: *The Coaching Habit: Say Less, Ask More & Change the Way You Lead Forever,* by Michael Bungay Stanier, is a great resource. You learn not only what questions to ask of your team but also how to ask them. Too many of us add extraneous words and sentences around the question resulting in confusion. Then we get upset because the person does not answer the question. Stanier offers a great quotation from Clayton Christensen in his book, "Without a good question, a good answer has no place to go." We need to ask questions of everyone in our life. That is how we build relationships and our knowledge base. Consider the types of questions that make you feel valued when someone reaches out to you or engages in a conversation. They are typically deep questions and contain a genuine sense of curiosity. The seven questions posed by Stanier allow you to build relationships and become a better coach for your team and, ultimately, a better leader. Consider the return of educators from summer break. Instead of simply asking, "How was your summer?" try asking, "What filled your bucket this summer?" or "Did you start any new hobbies or learn anything new this summer?" These types of questions show a desire to learn about the individual and show a sense of caring.

LISTEN: If you are going to ask a question, you might as well listen to the answer! Everyone wants to be heard. In a world full of distractibility, one of the most important gifts we can provide our team is our attention. If you are looking at your phone or computer while a team member is speaking to you, the message is clear: "I am not interested and stopped listening." By looking directly at the person speaking, taking notes, and asking questions, you are providing an opportunity to connect and build upon the relationship.

RESPECT EVERYONE UP AND DOWN THE CHAIN OF COMMAND: There has to be mutual respect within an organization in order to move forward. The leader has to demonstrate respect for all of their direct reports as well as all individuals. This occurs through messaging and tone as well as accessibility. Mid-level managers may find this even more difficult because they may not always agree with the decisions coming from the boss, yet have to deliver the news. It can be very easy to fall into the trap of telling your team the boss' idea is not good and you do not believe in it, but you have to do it. That undermines your boss and, in the long run, will undermine you because the lack of respect you are showing trickles down. Eventually, your subordinates will tell others when they do not agree with your ideas or perhaps question your role because you are not able to represent the employees in the trenches. We are aware of the many ways we can show respect to our colleagues, and it can be easy to let some of these slide when we are stressed or feeling overwhelmed. We can become short or terse in our responses. We might become more demanding in our requests or statements. These types of actions chip away at our relationships and they begin to fracture. Everyone in your organization deserves your respect, and if their actions suggest otherwise, consider if they should remain in your organization.

ACCEPT RESPONSIBILITY: As a leader, accept responsibility for what happens in the organization and on your team. This is part of leadership, and it needs to be acknowledged as well as lived. This means you need to actually state it, at times, in front of your team, "I am responsible for…" More importantly, accept when things go wrong. For example, "I am responsible for our team missing the deadline." You may not have been part of the planning or execution, but your team missed the deadline that was in place. As the leader, you should have been aware of the timetable and their ability to get the report to the Board or stakeholder. If you failed to check in, then you are responsible. If a teacher mishandles a disciplinary situation in their classroom, it is on you for not ensuring they understood the standard operating procedure. This aligns with the idea from Jocko Willink and Leif Babin in their book, *Extreme Ownership: How U.S. Navy SEALs Lead and Win*. Oftentimes, we want to point toward a subordinate who made the mistake. However, as the leader, you are responsible for making sure the subordinate understands the expectations.

WORK HARD AND COMPETE: Just about everyone you meet will tell you how hard they work. While some are providing an accurate assessment, many overestimate how hard they are working. This shows up in some conversations as a game of "misery poker." One teacher might talk about the number of tests they have to grade and how difficult it is, followed by a colleague chiming in with how much harder it is to grade papers than tests. It is a game of one-upmanship that no one wins in the end. The reality is that many of us have the ability to give more and do more, yet when left to our devices, we do not push ourselves to the level we are capable. This is why we need coaches, trainers, or mentors in our lives. As a leader, you must recognize this, and identify someone who will help to ensure you work hard to grow and improve consistently. In addition, when it comes to working hard, nothing will push you more than competition. Along with working hard each day, you should also compete with yourself. Are you getting better today or falling behind? There is no such thing as maintaining; you are either better or worse than the day before. By setting a standard for yourself and pushing yourself, your team will see what it means to work hard and compete. Finally, let them see you work, and never ask something of the team that you would not do yourself. Remember the All Blacks' philosophy: no one on the team is ever too big or too important to sweep the shed. Everyone on the team, including the captain and coaches, is responsible for cleaning the locker room after a training session or a match. As a school leader, community members will notice if you stop to pick up a piece of trash walking down the hall or if you choose to walk past it.

LIVE WITH INTEGRITY: At the end of the day, your integrity is all you have. There may be an opportunity to fool those around you, but you know, each night when you put your head down on your pillow, if you made decisions with integrity. It's important to recognize when you are in danger of stepping away from your values and your integrity. As Jocko Willink says, "Take the high ground or the high ground will take you."

Questions to ask yourself before/during/after difficult conversations or scenarios:

- Am I living my principles?
- Am I staying true to my core values that are important or do I just reference them when it is convenient?
- How do I respond when I recognize I'm falling short?

The ability to answer these questions truthfully will allow you to live with integrity. In chapter 3, I referenced the poem, *The Man in the Glass*, by (Peter) Dale Winbrow, Sr. This is the perfect time to review it again. If you are not familiar with it, I encourage you to look it up, read it and reflect upon the words. You are the only one who truly knows if you are living a life of integrity.

BE DECISIVE: Leaders need to make decisions every single day. These can have minor or major implications for your team and organization. Some decisions may require input from others, seek those team members out. There are other times when you already have the information necessary to make the decision. In any case, once you have the information available, make a decision, and communicate it to the team. If you are not ready because you need more information, notify the team and get to work on collecting the needed information. Simply waiting to see if the information comes forward or choosing not to make the decision often results in delays and questions around what is happening. Communicate the steps to your team and keep them informed. Resolute decision making leads to confidence and progress for you and your team.

TAKE A BALANCED APPROACH – RESPOND; DO NOT REACT: There are many ways to go about leading an organization or team. It is important that we remain balanced and strike the right tone with everyone in the organization. This includes daily interactions as well as the decisions we make. Using the analogy of golf, you have a club in your bag for just about every scenario. (That is true for most individuals; however, I am not one of them as they do not make clubs to hit your ball out of the water!) There are different approaches you will need to take based on which team member you are talking to or which task you are completing. By recognizing the need to be balanced, you are already starting to think bigger picture and look out and up. Similarly, we need to make a conscious decision to respond and not react to issues or people. A response entails recognition of what is happening through detachment and observation. A reaction happens when we do not allow ourselves time to process what is happening and allow our emotions to take the lead. It is rare that we find ourselves in situations where we have to react immediately. The more practice and experience you gain with detaching, the more quickly you may be able to respond. Again, a quick response may not always be necessary. You can let the team know that you will get back to them after you have a chance to gather more information or speak to the right people. As a school leader, your faculty and your parents will appreciate the fact that you are asking for more time to consider their request or look into their concern. Immediate reactions to issues often result in greater problems for all involved. The OODA Loop referenced in chapter 3 can help you in this regard as well.

ESTABLISH AND STRENGTHEN RELATIONSHIPS: You cannot lead if no one is willing to follow you. The only people who will follow are the ones you make connections with and build relationships with on a consistent basis. Relationships are maintained and strengthened with check-ins, conversations, and recognition of important events (weddings, births, funerals). Your team will give you everything they have if they know you care. You demonstrate this by clearly showing a commitment to the relationship. We are all busy and pulled in many directions. The simple check-in here and there can go a long way in helping to maintain the connections that are necessary to sustain the organization. We talked earlier in the book about the importance of questions and being curious. This is how you grow the connections with your team and show your commitment to them. I encourage you to schedule your check-ins and attendance at games or performances. If you do not put these items on your calendar, they will not be a priority and could fall to the wayside. This will have a direct impact on your relationships in the community.

DO YOUR HOMEWORK AND BE PREPARED: As you enter a leadership role or prepare for an important meeting with other team leaders, always do your homework. I referenced the Goldsmith quotation earlier when addressing new leaders and it remains equally as important in this section of the book. You cannot rely on what you did previously if you want to be successful in your new role as a leader. You must be prepared for the questions that will be asked of you and the scenarios that will unfold. This does not mean you will have all the answers, nor does it mean you should refrain from asking questions. That said, there are aspects of your role that you should know about, including how meetings run, the general meeting culture, email etiquette, and so on. Being humble requires asking questions and bringing an open mind, but if it appears you truly have no idea what is happening, that will sink your leadership right away. Put the time and energy in on the front end.

THE IMPORTANCE OF COMMUNICATION: As a varsity boys' lacrosse coach, I was fond of telling the team "communication alleviates confusion." A lot can happen in the course of the game, and as the coach, we cannot be on the field with the players. We need to do our best coaching in practice and let the players take care of the rest on game day. It was important for them to understand that the seven players (goalie + six field players) working together on defense had to communicate with one another in order to be successful. If only four or five players know the defensive call in a given scenario, we are likely going to lose out and allow the other team to score. The more we communicate, the less confusion exists among the team and the greater chance of success. As I translate that to my work with faculty as a school leader, I consider this quotation from Al Golden, former Head Football Coach of Temple University and the University of Miami, "In the absence of communication, there is darkness and the unknown. We are limited in what we can do there." Like children who envision monsters in their bedroom when there is no nightlight, adults also create images in their mind when they are in the dark at work. If we do not communicate a new policy or protocol clearly, it leaves a void or darkness. Adults will often fill this void with their own ideas or information. They may even begin sharing their ideas with colleagues and you have now lost control of the message. Do not leave your team in the dark!

> *One way to help alleviate these issues is to always ask and answer three questions of yourself:*
> *What do I know?*
> *Who else needs to know it?*
> *Have I told them?*

People want to know what is happening in the organization and what decisions are being made. In most cases, they want to be a part of the thought process or decision making process. Too often, we take this for granted or think we have communicated enough. Each day, as you take in new information, ask yourself those three questions. It is possible you may not need to share any information at that moment but unlikely. There are going to be team members who need to help institute a new policy or support a top-down decision. Keep them informed and get some feedback from them. If there needs to be a school wide announcement, consider the best way to communicate it and how quickly it must take place. This sort of transparent communication is appreciated by the team and lets them know that you value their contributions and want them to be involved.

ALWAYS STRIVE TO BE CLEAR AND CONCISE: In considering the Al Golden quotation a second time, we must realize that what we leave open for interpretation will be interpreted as each individual wishes. If team members leave a meeting and each of them has their own interpretation of the next steps, that is the fault of the leader. Before asking yourself why they can't follow guidelines or wonder how they possibly did not get the message, reflect on what you shared and how you shared it. You must be clear on what needs to happen for the success of the mission. In the same vein, be concise and keep it simple. There is no need to overcomplicate issues. For the most part, it is about the mission and providing clear guidance or objectives. If there are constraints or limits that you want in place, state them. If necessary, explain the constraints. If one paragraph can summarize the message, then write one paragraph. If it can be bullet points, use bullet points. Provide an easy way for the team to understand the message you want to convey. Finally, take the next step to ensure understanding.

ENSURE THE MESSAGE IS UNDERSTOOD AND REPORTING LINES ARE CLEAR: George Bernard Shaw stated, "The single biggest problem in communication is the illusion that it has taken place." It is your role as the leader to alleviate this problem. Whether you assign a specific task with specific steps to complete or you give your team autonomy to complete the task, make it a point to know if everyone understands the task. Brief backs are one way to ensure understanding. The other is for the team member to tell you how they will know the mission is complete.

- **PRACTICE BREIF BACKS (US ARMY RETIRED GENERAL GEORGE CASEY) -** after delivering the message, ask for it to be repeated back to you. Once the task is complete, ask for an explanation on the objective and how it was reached.
- **"PAINT IT DONE FOR ME." (BRENÉ BROWN) -** assign a task and ask for an explanation of what complete or finished will look like.

DELIVER MESSAGES IN MULTIPLE MODALITIES:

Inevitably there will be team members in the organization who prefer communication in different forms. Some will want to hear it stated directly while others want to read an email, and still others will want to hear you while looking at a diagram or spreadsheet. By using multiple modalities to deliver your message, you are hitting all of the individuals in your organization. If it is important enough to take time away from individuals to have a meeting, then you should do everything you can to ensure the team members understand the message being delivered.

- **UTILIZE THE WRITTEN WORD:** speak directly about the topic and provide slides or diagrams as part of a presentation
- **WHEN SPEAKING, BE MINDFUL OF CADENCE, TONE AND VOLUME:** Your team is listening and watching you lead. They are paying attention to your emails, your phone or zoom calls and, especially, how you present in a meeting format. From the opening sentence or statement, your team has a sense of the

direction you are going and how you plan to get there. The way you share written or verbal responses to questions sends a message to each team member. If you close by delegating tasks or assignments, you better have their attention. Do your homework, and be prepared. Detach from the work you are doing around crafting the message, and look at it with a critical lens: How would I respond to this message? What do I think of the cadence, tone and volume of the delivery? **Chao breeds chaos, calm breeds calm.**

IF IT IS IMPORTANT ENOUGH TO SAY ONCE, REPEAT IT:

Everyone in your organization should be able to state and identify the team mission, vision, and values. It should not matter what their role is in the school or organization because everyone needs to pull in the same direction in order to be successful. If you or your teammates cannot easily recall the mission, for example, it is likely too wordy or confusing. That is a problem. We all need to know the North Star for our organization for two reasons. The first is that the mission, vision, and values are the driving force behind every decision and action you make. The second reason is that the individual purpose for each faculty member should align with the school's. If that is not the case, the individual should seek opportunities elsewhere. We begin every school year talking about the mission and values of the school while also talking about our own purpose or why. This helps to frame our work together and also with our students. The mission, vision, and core values should be repeated consistently along with the messages that support each of them.

LIVE, STATE, AND RESTATE THE MISSION AND VISION OF THE ORGANIZATION: It is easy to get lost in the day-to-day activities of the organization, and this is especially true in schools. As leaders, we can find ourselves rushing from one fire to the next in a reactionary mode. We all have some days that are more challenging than others for any number of reasons. We are able to persevere and demonstrate resilience when we focus on our purpose and our why. The mission and the vision of the organization should be clear and easy for you and your team to recall. This way you can consider the impact of your decision in the context of the mission. If you are seeking to develop respectful citizens, then you can use that knowledge in determining how to move forward with a student who made a derogatory comment in class or on social media. It helps frame the conversation with both the aggrieved student and the student responsible for the comment. If the mission statement is a long, text heavy statement, it is likely easily forgotten or, worse yet, ignored. It may lead to confusion, and people may develop their own interpretations because nothing is clear. Revisit the mission and vision often and talk about it with your team. Emphasize the why behind it and ask others to do the same.

LISTEN WITH THE INTENT TO UNDERSTAND: As a leader, it is your job to listen to your people and to support them on a daily basis. This is not possible if you are only listening to rebut the idea or suggestions of your team members or direct reports. As you listen to them, write down what they are saying as a sign of your willingness to listen. It also helps you keep a record of the conversation and hold yourself accountable. It is important that you follow up with this person to provide an update on what information you gathered based on their questions, concerns or suggestions. This shows your commitment to them as an individual. You may not always be able to address the issue as they want or as they see fit, but listening and putting in the effort to find out more builds trust and respect. During the conversation, ask questions that dive deeper. Active listening is more than nodding or saying yes. Ask clarifying questions, or repeat what they said to ensure you understand it. Ask them what steps they have taken to resolve the issue. Be careful not to just offer advice or try to fix the issue. If you fix everyone else's problems, they will keep coming back to you, and worse, you will not be able to dedicate time to the larger goals and needs of the organization. There is a delicate balance between giving your time and protecting your time. Two ideas to consider around listening:

- Listen to understand and not to rebut/respond
- Prepare for conversations and prepare questions ahead of time - refer to *The Coaching Habit: Say Less, Ask More & Change the Way You Lead* by Michael Bungay Stanier who has seven questions to consider:
    - What's on your mind?
    - What else?
    - What's the real challenge here for you?
    - What do you really want?
    - How can I help?
    - If you say yes now, what are you saying no to later?
    - What was most useful aspect of our conversation?

DELIVERING FEEDBACK: Everyone needs feedback, and they need it consistently. This should be delivered in both one-on-one and group settings. When delivering positive feedback, be specific, especially, in a group setting. Identify what work or task was done well and how, so it can be repeated. The general platitude of "Great job, Bill," does not help anyone and is quickly forgotten. Instead of this approach, point to a specific example of what Bill did that was noteworthy. This shows that you are paying attention and also lets Bill know why the action was deserving of praise. When delivering constructive feedback that can be perceived as negative, it should always be given individually, never in a group. Before giving any feedback to your team member, ask the individual how they feel the project is going or how they felt after writing the report. If the task is complete, ask if there are areas to improve moving forward. By taking this approach, you are holding up a mirror for them to reflect instead of giving your opinions. In the conversation, you might get them to provide their own constructive feedback based on the reflection. This often leads to growth and internal desire to improve. Instead of being told where a mistake occurred, the team member finds it on their own, which is more likely to result in change. This is easier for some people than others, and you may need to provide more direct feedback depending on the individual. Consider utilizing some of the ideas below when it is time to give feedback.

- Deliver it in the moment, do not wait.
    - If it seems hard now, it will only be harder later.
- Acknowledge your role in the problem.
    - "I failed to clearly explain…"

- - "I failed to give you the resources or time to…"
- Escalate feedback as needed.
  - "What do you need to hit the objective next time?"
  - "What can I do to ensure you understand the objective or the goal?"
- Giving praise.
  - Be mindful of how frequent you give it - not too often, but be wary of never giving any.
  - Be specific - identify individuals over teams, and identify the specific area.

"People don't care how much you know until they know how much you care."
- Teddy Roosevelt

In chapter four, we took several of the principles discussed earlier in the book and showed how they could be utilized as part of your leadership strategies. It is important to note that strong leaders use these principles throughout their daily experiences and life. You cannot be a good leader if you only implement these principles at certain times. NBA legend, Kobe Bryant, stated,

> … if you want to be excellent at something, you have to be excellent all the time. It's a way of life; you can't just show up on Monday and be excellent. No, it don't work that way. You gotta be excellent across the board. That's how you build habits. Excellence becomes a habit and that's just who you are.

In other words, you cannot be a great leader when it is convenient or when you feel like it. To be a truly great leader in your community, espouse the principles found in this book consistently. If you choose to act with integrity only some of the time or to be humble when it suits you, then you are not living by those principles. It cannot be a *sometimes* approach. You develop these principles through listening and asking questions. These principles can be learned and strengthened over time as you practice them consistently.

EXAMPLE:

PRINCIPLE: Delivering feedback with the intent to listen for understanding.

WHAT I DID BEFORE: When I asked a team member or direct report to come to my office for a meeting, I did not always provide the topic or reason in advance. We started the meeting by exchanging pleasantries about family or thoughts on work, then I told them we had to talk about a recent parent interaction that I had heard about. They were caught off guard by the topic and became defensive throughout the conversation. I told them what I had heard from the family and, when they shared their perspective, I pointed out the contradictions to the parent's version of events. The meeting ended with me asking the team member to take a different approach in the future, which they agreed to try and do so. Neither one of us felt great after the exchange as it was not about trust and relationships. It was about a top-down expectation from me to the faculty member.

WHAT I WANT TO DO DIFFERENTLY: I want to schedule the meeting and share the topic in advance. I want the team member to reflect on their interaction with the parent before, during, and after the meeting. I would like for them to know that I understand their perspective and that I am here to support them. I want to engage in meaningful dialogue that strengthens our relationship and helps them grow as a member of our community.

HOW WILL I ACCOMPLISH THIS:

- I will invite my team member to my office for a meeting and let them know we are discussing a parent concern so they can be prepared.
- I will ask my team member to reflect on the interaction in advance of our meeting.
- I will put my own notes and questions to ask together in an organized fashion and remind myself that I am here to listen and hold up a mirror.
- When the meeting begins, I will ask the team member to share their perspective on the interaction.
- I will ask clarifying questions throughout and support my team member as they reflect on the scenario.
- I will ask them to share their thoughts on how to address similar situations in the future.

QUESTIONS TO CONSIDER:

- Who can give you honest and helpful feedback on a consistent basis?
- Do you accept responsibility at all times?

- Is your decision making grounded in integrity?
- Have you established the right relationships, and are you maintaining them?
- Are you specific and consistent in your feedback?

CHAPTER 5
FITNESS PRINCIPLES

Heading straight from college into the workforce meant that I brought some positive habits and not so positive habits with me. As a high school and college athlete, working out had been a part of my life for a long time. Starting my career at a boarding school meant I had access to a track, weight room, and fields on a daily basis. I was also single and could pick and choose when to workout based on my teaching and coaching schedule. My eating habits were not the best, and I often just chose the most appealing items from the dining hall with no consideration of health content. Time on the weekends was spent playing club lacrosse and enjoying time at the bar afterward with teammates and friends. After changing schools and taking on greater responsibility, I allowed myself to rationalize choices. I was too busy to workout now or did not have time to play club lacrosse anymore. I would bring work home every night and was not always focused on my family or relationships, often blaming the work. There was always an excuse for why I could not do more or take steps to improve my overall fitness: mental, physical and spiritual. Much of what has been written in this book coincided with a change in my approach to daily life.

LEAVE WORK AT WORK: This is challenging for many individuals who feel compelled to stay connected to work at all hours. I have been guilty of this for much of my career. It became increasingly difficult during the first part of the COVID pandemic when people began working from home and the boundaries became even more blurred. The evolution of technology has made everyone accessible 24/7, and there is a sense that you are not doing your job if you are not accessible to the same degree as your colleagues or competitors. The reality is that very little has to get done outside of work hours. I recognize there will be emergencies that occur which require the attention of leaders, but they are far fewer than we let ourselves believe. It is your job as a leader to establish a culture in your organization that acknowledges the importance and expectation of hard work during working hours so that off-hours can be just that, off. Do not send late-night emails or texts that require an immediate response. Model the importance of leaving work behind so you can focus on yourself and your family. When we are preoccupied with work at all hours staring at a screen, texting, or engaging in a work-related phone call, we are not available to anyone else including ourselves. Develop a ritual at the end of the day that signifies the closing of the workday - organize your desk, make a list for the following day, turn on your away phone message, whatever. Create a sense of closure to the day and allow yourself to move onto the next part of the day with your family.

READ EVERY DAY: Books are said to be windows or mirrors, and I wholeheartedly believe that statement. Each book provides an opportunity to learn something new about yourself or the world around you. It is not possible for us to experience every scenario that can impact our personal or professional lives, but we can read the stories of others and learn from them. As General James Mattis stated, "Thanks to my reading, I have never been caught flat-footed by any situation, never at a loss for how any problem has been addressed (successfully or unsuccessfully) before. It doesn't give me all the answers, but it lights what is often a dark path ahead."

We have an opportunity to be prepared for whatever tomorrow brings based on our decision to read. On the surface, it can be easy to point to the full day you already have and state there is no time for reading. I argue that putting in the time to read will save you more time in the long run, based on what James Mattis shared. You are putting in the time on the front end instead of trying to reinvent the wheel in the moment. I encourage you to evaluate how you spend your available time when not working. Reading in preparation for your work is important, but it is also healthy to read topics that do not have anything to do with work or your professional life as it allows your mind to focus on something else. You can immerse yourself in a faraway land and leave the daily stressors of life behind. Make it a point to set aside time every day to read. Whether you wake up 15 minutes early or go to bed earlier in the evening, set aside time to read. Similar to many working parents, I wrongly believed that time to read did not exist. I made the same statement about exercise. When I stopped to look at my schedule, I recognized that I was wasting time watching TV and not actively growing or developing as a person. I decided it was a better use of my time to read more and started to practice this consistently in 2016. I began taking notes and would build a list of books to share out with people at the end of the year. I wanted to share what I learned and also remind people of the benefits of reading. I wanted other leaders to see that it is possible to dedicate time to do this.

PRACTICE GRATITUDE EVERY DAY IN WORD AND DEED (WRITE IT AND SPEAK IT): Happy people are not more grateful; grateful people tend to be happier. *Positive Psychology* references multiple studies that have shown how gratitude increases happiness. Researchers Dr. Robert A. Emmons and Dr. Michael E. McCullough, conducted a study on gratitude asking individuals to write a few sentences on gratitude for 10 weeks. They found participants were more hopeful about the future and exercised more. They also had fewer medical appointments. People do not suddenly find joy and happiness and thus start to appreciate all that is around them and all that they have. Once we recognize that what we have is enough and we become grateful, we become happier. You will abandon the search for what is next...the next car, the big house, the promotion. A sense of knowing that what we have in our life brings us happiness and joy. Every morning after exercising, I journal about the events from the previous day, both professional and personal. I want to reflect on my experiences so I can grow as a leader, parent, and husband. I end this reflection with one question, "What am I grateful for today?" I then write three bullet points in response to the question. I strongly encourage others to develop a similar daily routine. Some people choose the morning to kick start their day, as I do. Others may choose to practice their gratitude before going to sleep as a way to end the day. Writing it out makes you think about it, and it also helps you to develop a mindset of gratitude. It is also important to practice it with your family, acknowledging gratitude at the dinner table or while getting kids ready for bed. A simple question can be, "What happened today that you are grateful for?" This allows us to shift our mindset from challenge to opportunity. It also helps your children see they have more than they realize. I started the practice several years ago, and I have seen it impact my words and actions. As a lifelong Buffalo Bills fan, I have suffered through many frustrating seasons. At one point, the Bills took a positive trajectory and made the playoffs in 2017, which was the first time since 1999! A colleague texted me congrats after the Bills clinched the spot. I wrote a text back stating the season was only extended by a week and they would soon be out of the playoffs, but before hitting send, I deleted the text and rewrote, "Thanks. Can't wait for them to win this week and then head to New England to roll Brady and the Pats!" It did not go as planned as gratitude does not help you control or predict the future, but it does give you control over your mindset and perspective. It also has allowed me to enjoy a few more successful seasons for the Bills including the AFC East title in 2020 which was the first since the mid 90s!

CHOOSE ENTHUSIASM OVER APATHY: Anyone can be apathetic, it takes zero effort and allows individuals to forgo taking any responsibility for how they feel or act. It is always someone else's fault, and there is nothing anyone can do to alter it. That mindset gets individuals nowhere in life and leaves them feeling lonely, as others do not want to be around people who act this way. Enthusiasm requires effort and an attitude that you are capable of making change, whatever the circumstances. We all need to put our best foot forward, and attack the day with an enthusiastic mindset. It is contagious for those who also want to get better and work hard. There will be detractors, and you have to be mindful of them. These are unhappy, apathetic people who want to pull you down like the crabs at the bottom of the steam pot.

When the crabs begin to steam, the ones on top try to crawl out, and the ones beneath will pull them back down. This creates an environment where everyone pulls the other person down to their level. That can manifest in a few different ways in schools. You may hear questions such as: why is she so happy? What does he have that I do not that makes him so enthusiastic? These are people who are not committed to bettering themselves or others. Furthermore, they do not want you to be successful nor improve. Every day, we are presented with a new opportunity and must choose to accept it in a way that will be fun, engaging and make you and those around you better.

SET ASIDE TIME FOR PHYSICAL EXERCISE: According to the Mayo Clinic, exercise provides multiple benefits such as an increase in energy levels, improved mood, better sleep, and can also limit your risk of health problems such as stroke, certain types of cancer, diabetes, and depression to name a few. The bottom line is that exercise is directly connected to a better, healthier life. There is time in the day for this just like there is time for reading, but you must make the commitment. I recognize everyone has their own internal clock and has optimum hours of operation. It is my experience that most people who do not want to exercise in the morning simply do not have the discipline to get up and do the work. The excuse is that the morning is too rushed and there is more time or flexibility in the afternoon or evening. The reality is that we do not have more time at any one point during the day, and, as the day goes on, more people are pulling at our time and scheduling our time for us. This is certainly true in my case with a family of five, a full schedule that prevents any midday exercise and family obligations in the evening or an unexpected work responsibility. With this in mind, I have made the commitment to wake up in the morning 90 minutes before anyone else in my house. This allows me to have an uninterrupted workout, complete breathing exercises or meditation, and write. I am in control and have ownership of that time. I understand that everyone will not want to get up significantly earlier than usual. By taking small steps, such as waking up 15 minutes early to stretch and practice yoga, or by completing some form of this in the evening, you will see improvement. The hardest step is often the first. Once we commit and develop the habit, it becomes routine.

PRACTICE A FORM OF MINDFULNESS DAILY: Mindfulness provides space in your day and in your life. It allows you to be present. It requires practice and effort that likely will not give you immediate feedback or results. That makes it even more difficult to develop the habit. For some individuals, mindfulness can be found through meditation. There are some great apps that you can use to help you get started. *Headspace* is one example and is free for K-12 educators. If meditation is not for you, the app also offers simple breathing exercises. No matter your preference, each of us needs to build in time for this important practice.

SEEK MODERATION IN ALL CHOICES: Our culture and society in the US have a strong foundation in alcohol going all the way back to the American Revolution and the founding of this country. The *important* conversations were happening in taverns. The cue to imbibe is a social gathering. Regardless of the latest studies on how much alcohol is "OK" to have, it is imperative to recognize the role alcohol plays in your life and how it impacts those around you. Dr. Peter Attia shared, on a podcast with Tim Ferris, that we should not drink just because it is there. When we do this, and when we drink in excess, we can damage our overall mental and physical health. We may also damage relationships that are important in our lives. We need to be our best as school leaders and limiting our consumption of alcohol is a necessary step in this direction.

Some individuals avoid alcohol but may indulge in unhealthy treats. Perhaps it is stopping on the drive home at a fast food restaurant, or maybe after dinner, it's the pint of Ben and Jerry's that seems to be a single serving but really isn't! When we use food to level out our emotions or as a source to unwind, it becomes a crutch. Whenever we are facing a challenge or feeling stress, we will seek it out and, before we know it, moderation is no longer an option. Our health and well-being takes a hit, and we cannot be our best self when needed.

Before I began my nightly reading habit, I watched plenty of TV. This probably goes back to my days as a latch-key kid. I would often stay up late during the week to watch games or sitcoms, which would make for difficult mornings. I might binge some shows on the weekends and stay up late resulting in a loss of sleep. When we seek refuge in TV, movies or social media, it can come at a cost. I am not suggesting you avoid all of it all the time but that you are intentional in what you are consuming, and understand why you are doing it. A comedy on Netflix might be just what you need after a long week, but what are you doing afterwards? Is it another movie or show? Is it social media scrolling to see what you missed while you were watching the movie?

Each example above shows how we can step off the path and lose focus. Whether it is drinking, eating, bingeing Netflix shows or social media, none of it is helping you grow. Be mindful and intentional with your choices - know how you are spending your time and why.

FIND A HIGHER PURPOSE: When we only live for ourselves and do not recognize a higher purpose in our lives, we often make choices that are in our best interest only and rarely think of others. For some, this may mean practicing religion. Whatever your religious viewpoint, you know what it means to be considerate of others and put them before yourselves. You recognize that life is about more than just you. There is a guiding star that helps in your decision making. You may choose not to practice a religion, but there needs to be something that drives you to be better each day. As educators, you may be driven to provide greater opportunities for your students, or perhaps your teachers if you are a school leader. What is the higher purpose you are serving and why? This is an integral question because it forces you to think about your choices, not just in the moment but in the long term as well. How are your choices impacting those around you?

BE INTENTIONAL ABOUT SLOWING DOWN WHEN POSSIBLE: Everyone is facing different challenges in their daily life. We have different jobs, different responsibilities and take different approaches to address challenges. Some school leaders cannot tend to their own needs when they get up in the morning due to family obligations. Some have greater responsibilities at home than others. Each person has their own path and set of obstacles to navigate every day.

There are people on your team whose jobs ebb and flow depending on the calendar, which can lead to busy seasons. For example, your registrar will have quiet periods and busy periods during the school year. Be sure to know what your team's experience is and provide additional support to them. Likewise, take care of yourself in order to be the best leader you can. It is important to set aside the time to evaluate your weekly, monthly, and yearly calendar. Where are the moments that you can build in time to slow down, take a breath and give attention elsewhere?

It is too easy and, quite frankly, an excuse to say, "I do not have time." Everyone is working with the same 24 hours a day, 7 days a week, 365 days a year; it is about how you use your time. Block out time on your calendar when you can detach and take a 30,000-mile look at the life you are leading.

- Is it meaningful?
- Are you doing your best in your various roles? What can you do differently?
- Where are you in your personal life?
- Are you engaging in your meaningful relationships or are you taking them for granted?

Once you develop this skill, work with your team members on doing the same. Give them the gift of time one afternoon to ask themselves these questions and talk through their answers. Model the importance of slowing down, reflecting and engaging in meaningful dialogue. We all need to schedule time for this. As noted by the philosopher, Ferris Bueller, "Life moves pretty fast. If you don't stop and look around once in a while, you could miss it."

NEVER LOWER THE BAR FOR YOURSELF – BE ACCOUNTABLE TO YOU, THE PERSON IN THE MIRROR: It is important that we strive to be our best every day because we cannot make it up tomorrow or the next day. We only get one shot at each day. I will reiterate John Wooden's idea to his players here: You have to give 100% every day. Whatever you don't give, you can't make up for tomorrow. If you give only 75% today, you cannot give 125% tomorrow to make up for it. We all have days when we are not feeling our best, and perhaps our best effort will not match that of the previous day or week. That is understandable, so you do what you can on that day to the best of your ability. When the day comes to an end and you look in the mirror as you brush your teeth, ask yourself if you gave it your best. Answer honestly, and if you came up short, consider how you will improve tomorrow. Each day is a new opportunity to be our best, and we need to attack the day with that mindset. Depending on your schedule and that of your family, you might only see them briefly before you leave for work and they deserve your best. You might be an early riser who heads to work before the family is up. When you return home from a difficult day, those people, who have not seen you in 12+ hours, deserve your best. The faculty member who rarely gets to meet with you one-on-one deserves your best in that given meeting on that particular day. Hold yourself accountable to be the best you can each and every day. Evaluate yourself, and learn from the day's actions or events through reflection.

JOURNAL AND REFLECT: It is important to reflect often on your experiences so you can learn and make different choices in the future. It provides an opportunity to hold yourself accountable as you write down all that happened in the previous day, week or month. You are able to answer questions that you may not have given time or thought to in the past. Everyone's journal is going to be a little different, and so is their approach. For me, writing a daily reflection on the previous day helps me recognize areas that went well and areas that need to improve. It also allows me to include my daily gratitude: What are three things in life I am grateful for today?

> **"We do not learn from experience; we learn from reflecting on experience."**
> *- John Dewey.*

Each morning after I exercise, I sit down to write my daily reflection from the previous day. It is important for output to occur before input which is why I write prior to checking email and social media. I want to get my thoughts out before someone else tries to infiltrate my head. In addition to this, my weekly reflection allows me to revisit goals from the previous week, along with things like interactions with colleagues, tasks completed and tasks not yet complete. It serves as a reflective moment and a planning period. I can see where I am spending my time and if I need to change that. I typically write Saturday morning about the previous week to help me reflect and plan for the upcoming week. I can make plans based on what I observed in my reflection. In monthly reflections, I look for patterns and also revisit goals once again. I choose to write at the start of every month. This can fluctuate based on my schedule, but I work to ensure it does not go beyond the fourth or fifth day of the next month. Everyone should journal in a way that makes sense to them. I still have to revisit the why and how of my reflections and appreciate reading the suggestions and examples of others. Here are some questions to help you get started:

- Potential questions for your reflections
    - What wins did I have this week?
    - What am I grateful for?
    - What is important to me and how am I demonstrating it?
    - Who helped me this week? Did I thank them?
    - What is hidden from plain sight?
    - Step back and consider the entire chess board.
    - What choices should I revisit this week? Why?
    - Am I acting above the line or below the line?

As you think about your fitness and well-being, recognize that many of our greatest leaders believe in the importance of these actions. Two examples of this are shared in the acronyms below:

- **REST** - Retired Army General George Casey
    - **R**ead, **E**xercise, **S**leep, **T**hink: We all feel a need to support our families and those we work with. Yet we cannot give everyone what they need if we are not taking care of ourselves. Think of the rules regarding the application of the oxygen mask every time we

fly. Put on your mask first, and then help your child because if you are not healthy and able to support the individuals in your life, who will? In addition, by taking the time to read and think about your personal and professional life, you not only grow as a person and leader, you also help those around you.

- **ARSENAL** - Dr. Dick Thompson
  - **A**wareness, **R**est, **S**upport, **E**xercise, **N**utrition, **A**ttitude, **L**earn: This acronym from Dr. Dick Thompson takes the REST idea a few steps further and expands on what should happen to take care of yourself and your team.

"We are not imprisoned by our circumstances, by luck or by unfairness in life. Not by crushing set-backs, self-inflicted mistakes or past success. We are not imprisoned by the times in which we live, by the number of hours in a day or even the number of hours we're granted in our short lives. In the end, we can control only a tiny sliver of what happens to us. But even so, we are free to choose, free to become great by choice."
- Jim Collins

All of the teams you lead or are a member of rely on you every day to be at your best. This is not possible if you are not utilizing a fitness mindset. This includes physical, mental, and spiritual. In order to invest in yourself, you need to invest the time. Step back and evaluate how you are using the time allotted to you each and every day. Where can you add 15 minutes of reading into your schedule? What can you take out of your schedule that is not adding value to your day or to your growth as a leader? We all have obligations and responsibilities that impact our schedule and how we use our time. We also have control over other aspects of our day. Earlier in the chapter, I noted that I prefer working out in the morning. I choose to do this because I know I do not have any responsibility from 4:30-5:45 each morning. My family, including the dogs, are all asleep during this time. By 5:45 someone, or a dog, is starting to rustle around and will need my attention. This was not always the case before we had children and dogs. I used to get up at 5:30 to exercise, and this has shifted earlier and earlier to accommodate for my responsibilities at home. Likewise, I used to be up late in the evenings seeking some quiet and solitude, but now that I am getting up earlier, I need to go to bed earlier. These are shifts and changes I have made so I can ensure I am finding the time for my own fitness. Every morning after working out, I set aside the time to write in my daily journal adding my gratitude for the day. This helps to frame my mental approach and mindset for the day after I have focused on my physical fitness. Each of us has our own unique schedule and opportunity to focus on fitness. If we make excuses and rationalize why we do not have time, we will only become weaker as leaders and individuals. We will burn out and fail our teams. If you remain committed to these habits and choices, you will find yourself overcoming more challenges and obstacles in your life both personally and professionally

EXAMPLE:

PRINCIPLE: Exercising

WHAT I DID BEFORE: I did not exercise regularly because I did not believe I had the time. I had a busy schedule and a family, and being a school leader demanded too much of my time and attention during working hours. I believed there was no time for my own fitness because all of it was devoted to others.

WHAT I WANT TO DO DIFFERENTLY: I want to build in time to exercise so I can be healthier, physically and mentally. I want to increase my energy levels and how I feel each day.

HOW WILL I ACCOMPLISH THIS:

- I will review my schedule and identify the time of day when I can begin with 15 minutes of exercise, something like walking, jogging, biking, or yoga.
- I will pick an activity to start that works for me and my schedule and understand I may need to be flexible.
- Once I have a plan in place I will build the habit by making it easier to complete
    - Set my alarm earlier and have workout clothes ready to go.
    - Pack a bag the night before work that I take with me to stop at the gym on the way home.
- I will find an accountability partner to help me succeed in my goal to improve my physical fitness.

QUESTIONS TO CONSIDER:

- Are you living a lifestyle that you are proud of?
- Are you exercising as often and as intensely as you should?
- When is the last time you read consistently in an effort to learn and grow?
- Do you actively reflect on the decisions, choices, and experiences happening in your life?
- Do you practice gratitude on a daily basis?
- When are you at your best mentally and physically?
    - How can you grow or build off of this?
- When do you feel weakest mentally and physically?
    - How can you avoid or limit this?

CHAPTER 6
DECISION MAKING

We are faced with decisions every day of our lives, some more difficult than others. Some become automated through habits such as brushing our teeth or having a second cup of coffee in the morning. Others are more complex and, potentially, impact more than just ourselves. That said, we can use mental models for all of our decision making in order to strengthen our process. Shane Parrish and his team at Farnam Street provide a variety of mental models and explain the importance of each. We may already use some of these models, but sometimes we choose the models that will give us the answer we want instead of the best answer. Each of the models below can be applied to different decisions. I encourage you to consider how each one might impact a decision you are making for yourself or those in your life.

MENTAL MODELS AS DEFINED BY FARNAM STREET:

- Mental models are how we understand the world. Not only do they shape what we think and how we understand, but they shape the connections and opportunities that we see. Mental models are how we simplify complexity, why we consider some things more relevant than others and how we reason.

- A mental model is simply a representation of how something works. We cannot keep all of the details of the world in our brains, so we use models to simplify the complex into understandable and in organized chunks.

SOME EXAMPLES:

- **Circle of Competence**
    - Be honest in delineating between what you actually know and what you think you know. Our ego drives us to make decisions based on what we think, and that can create more problems for everyone. By being vulnerable and allowing those with different knowledge or more knowledge than you provide input, you will get to the best solution possible.
    - "You have to figure out what your own aptitudes are. If you play games where other people have the aptitudes and you don't, you're going to lose. And that's as close to certain as any prediction that you can make. You have to figure out where you've got an edge. And you've got to play within your own circle of competence." C. Munger

- **1st Principles Thinking**
    - Break down complex problems into smaller, simpler parts before you reassemble from the ground up. It removes extraneous information and allows you to focus on the essentials.
    - Use Socratic questioning or try asking "5 Whys" to get to a solution
    - Reasoning by first principles is useful when you are 1) doing something for the first time, 2) dealing with complexity, and 3) trying to understand a situation with which you're having problems. In all of these areas, your

thinking gets better when you stop making assumptions and you stop letting others frame the problem for you.

- **Second-Order Thinking**
    - Too often, we solve one problem, only to create a new one because we are not looking far enough ahead. Ray Dalio, founder of Bridgewater Associates and author of *Principles: Life & Work*, shares his thoughts on the importance of second-order thinking: "Failing to consider second- and third-order consequences is the cause of a lot of painfully bad decisions, and it is especially deadly when the first inferior option confirms your own biases. Never seize on the first available option, no matter how good it seems, before you've asked questions and explored."
        - Always ask, "And, then what?" This allows you to look into the future one day later, one month later or even years later.
        - You may not see immediate pay off with this decision, but using second-order thinking may show you a long term payoff down the road. For example - the first day of exercise or cutting desserts
- **Probabilistic Thinking**
    - Probabilistic thinking is trying to estimate, using some tools of math and logic, the

likelihood of any specific outcome occurring. It is one of the best tools we have to improve the accuracy of our decisions. In a world where each moment is determined by an infinitely complex set of factors, probabilistic thinking helps us identify the most likely outcomes which can make our decisions more precise and effective.

- Successfully thinking in shades of probability means roughly identifying what matters, coming up with a sense of the odds, doing a check on our assumptions, then making a decision. We can act with a higher level of certainty in complex, unpredictable situations.

- **Occam's Razor**
    - The simplest explanation is preferable to one that is more complex. Simple theories are easier to verify. Simple solutions are easier to execute.
    - We should never blindly follow the results of applying a mental model which logic, experience, or empirical evidence contradict.
        - When you hear hoofbeats behind you, you should think: horses, not zebras—unless you are out on the African savannah.
    - This is not a substitute for critical thinking
        - Remember that opting for simpler explanations still requires work. They may be easier to falsify but still require

effort. The simpler explanation, although having a higher chance of being correct, is not always true.
- When to apply it
    - Don't over complicate and stack a theory if a simpler explanation is available. Pare it down and prune the excess.

- **Hanlan's Razor**
    - Do not assume the worst intention in the actions of others. Understanding Hanlon's Razor helps us see the world in a more positive light, stops us from making negative assumptions, and improves relationships.
    - "Never ascribe to malice that which is adequately explained by incompetence." - Napoleon
    - Assume best intentions, think/act rationally, show empathy
        - Useful to avoid confirmation bias
    - Helps us reconcile communication barriers or interactions
        - Think about traveling in a foreign country and not knowing the language
    - Be wary of naiveté, as there may be malicious intent
        - Use logic, experience, and evidence when evaluating

- **Inversion**
  - It is not enough to think about difficult problems only one way. Think about them forward and backward. Inversion often forces you to uncover hidden beliefs about the problem you are trying to solve.
  - Avoiding stupidity is easier than seeking brilliance.
    - It does not always solve the problem but, many times, keeps us from creating more problems
  - Inversion helps improve your understanding of the problem
    - Ex: We want to be more innovative. Instead of listing all ways to promote innovation, think of all the obstacles to innovation and try to remove them.

"The most successful problem solvers spend mental energy figuring out what type of problem they are facing before matching a strategy to it, rather than jumping in with memorized procedures."
- David Epstein

We must make decisions every single day of our lives from the moment we are up in the morning until we put our head back down on the pillow. Many of the decisions you make on a daily basis will not have a large impact on those around you. Yet there are some that carry more weight and how you approach them is incredibly important. Shane Parrish and his team at Farnam Street shared a variety of mental models that I included in this book to support your decision making. I encourage you to have a list of these at the office and to consider reviewing them when faced with a difficult decision around hiring or firing or in preparation for a difficult conversation with a family member. As a leader, it is important to be prepared for all the scenarios that unfold in your school, and it is your responsibility to put in the work ahead of time.

EXAMPLE: Your math department chair informs you in a January meeting that she has accepted the same position at another school. You are now in a position of needing to hire a new chair.

PRINCIPLE (MENTAL MODEL): Second-order thinking

WHAT I DID BEFORE: I talked with Human Resources about getting a job description and posting the position right away. I knew that math chairs were hard to come by, especially once hiring season really picked up and felt rushed to start the search immediately before all the best candidates were gone. I did not think about all of the various steps or consequences that happen once we made a decision.

WHAT I WANT TO DO DIFFERENTLY: I want to take a deep breath and consider the impact of the chair leaving and the appropriate steps to take. I want to utilize second-order thinking principles to consider the potential outcomes. I want to find out how the department members feel about her departure and also find out what they hope to have in a new chair. I want to be timely in the posting of the position but not rush into it. I want to make sure my team and the department feel a part of the process and invested in the hire for the betterment of the institution. I will take the time to consider what happens if I hire an internal candidate versus an external candidate.

HOW WILL I ACCOMPLISH THIS:

- I will thank the chair for her years of service and ask her when we can inform the department. Ideally, we will be in agreement, but as the leader, I may need to ask for a meeting sooner. I will be considerate and pragmatic.
- I will meet with the outgoing chair to discuss the state of the department, what they think the department may need moving forward, and ask them for any suggestions on how the department can improve.
- I will offer to meet with each member of the department individually and conduct empathy interviews to gain a better understanding of their perspective on the needs of the department and new chair. I will also ask them if they are interested in the position.
- I will work with Human Resources and the Dean of Faculty to craft the job description and post it.
- I will spend time considering second- and third-order principles regarding the hiring of an internal or external candidate.

- After a thoughtful and deliberate process, I will hire the best candidate for the position.

QUESTIONS TO CONSIDER:
- How do you evaluate your decision making skills and tactics?
    - Do you look at the results or the process?

CONCLUSION

We all face challenges each day when we get out of bed, and how we approach these challenges will define the day. This begins with our mindset and the words we use. As I shared in the opening of the book, I prefer the word opportunity instead of challenge. There is an opportunity to learn and grow in every experience. We have the ability to choose to attack the day and make strides to improve or we can continue to drift and react to what is happening. People who let life happen to them and live without intention will not grow or improve and will live a life of regret. Individuals who want to get better can do so by following a set of principles. These serve as guard rails and help them remain focused. Identify two or three areas you want to improve: physical fitness, relationships, or work/life harmony, and set an intentional path. Use a journal or notebook to record your journey for the area and set goals. Be sure to include statements of gratitude in your journal as this will help tremendously with your mindset. Good luck in your path as a school leader, and know that you have people who support you and believe in you. They are waiting for you to take the next steps in becoming the best leader you can be. Are you ready for that opportunity?

GLOSSARY OF TERMS

5 Whys - When you have defined the problem, you ask the first why and generate as many answers as possible. For each answer, ask 4 more whys. The successive whys must be a response to the most recent answer. This allows for multiple lanes of inquiry and also gets to the root cause.

ARSENAL - acronym from Dr. Dick Thompson to evaluate your fitness; **Awareness, Rest, Support, Exercise, Nutrition, Attitude, Learn**

Brief Backs - a team member repeats back to the leader the mission he or she has been assigned to ensure understanding

Courage - the ability to make difficult decisions on a daily basis.

Detach - physically or mentally removing yourself from a situation so you can see the larger picture

Discipline - the ability to focus on what needs to be done versus what I want to do

Goals - desired outcomes or results

Gratitude - to show appreciation and thanks for what you have

Humility - living a life without arrogance or overt pride

Integrity - ability to make ethical and moral decisions on a consistent basis regardless of circumstances

Mental Models - a representation of how we can view the world and how we do view the world

Mitfreude - *with joy* when directly translated from German; finding joy in the success of others

Mudita - Sanskrit word that is equivalent to feeling joy for others; a sense of sympathetic or vicarious joy

Planning Fallacy - when you do not set aside enough time to complete the task; we often believe it will take less time than actually necessary to complete the task

Principles - guidelines or guard rails that connect your actions and behaviors to your values

REST - acronym from General Casey**: Rest, Exercise, Sleep, Think**

Root Cause - the actual cause of the problem as opposed to the superficial and often visible cause

Socratic Questioning - a disciplined approach to questioning in which you try to get the other person in the conversation to answer their own question(s). For example, "Have you thought of any other options?" "Why is this choice the best?" "How would you explain this decision to your team?"

Standards - actions or behaviors that guide our decision-making and support our goals.

Strategy - plan of action to achieve a specific outcome

Tactics - the day-to-day steps you take to implement your strategy and complete the mission

SUGGESTED READINGS TO FURTHER YOUR GROWTH AS A LEADER

Leadership

- *Extreme Ownership: How U.S. Navy SEALs Lead and Win* – Jocko Willink and Leif Babin
- *Dare to Lead: Brave Work. Tough Conversations. Whole Heart.* – Brené Brown
- *Great By Choice* – Jim Collins
- *Leadership Strategy and Tactics: Field Tactics* – Jocko Willink
- *Legacy: What the All Blacks Can Teach Us About the Business of Life* – James Kerr
- *Primal Leadership: Realizing the Power of Emotional Intelligence* – Annie McKee, Daniel Goleman, et al.
- *Principles: Life and Work* – Ray Dalio, Jeremy Bobb, et al.
- *Start with Why: How Great Leaders Inspire Everyone to Take Action* – Simon Sinek
- *The Effective Executive: The Definitive Guide to Getting Things Done* – Peter Drucker, Jim Collins, et al.
- *The Program: Lessons from Elite Military Units for Creating and Sustaining High-Performance Leaders and Teams* – Eric Kapitulik, Jake MacDonald, et al.

Personal Growth

- *Atomic Habits: An Easy & Proven Way to Build Good Habits & Break Bad Ones* – James Clear

- *Ego is the Enemy* – Ryan Holiday
- *Man's Search for Meaning* – Viktor E. Frankl, Simon Vance, et al.
- *Meditations* – Marcus Aurelius
- *The Power of Habit: Why We Do What We Do In Life and Business* – Charles Duhigg, Mike Chamberlain, et al.
- *The Choice: Escaping the Past and Embracing the Possible* – Dr. Edith Eva Egar, Tovah Feldshuh, et al.
- *Think Again: The Power of Knowing What You Don't Know* – Adam Grant
- *Tribe of Mentors: The Short Life Advice From the Best in the World* – Tim Ferris, Kaleo Griffith, et al.

Communication

- *Radical Candor: Be a Kick-Ass Boss Without Losing Your Humanity* – Kim Scott
- *The Power of Moments: Why Certain Experiences Have Extraordinary Impact* – Chip Heath, Dan Heath, et al.
- *The Coaching Habit: Say Less, Ask More & Change the Way You Lead Forever* – Michael Bungay Stanier, Daniel Maté, et al.
- *The Trillion Dollar Coach: The Leadership Playbook of Silicon Valley's Bill Campbell* - Eric Schmidt, Jonathan Rosenberg, et al.
- *You're Not Listening: What You're Missing and Why it Matters* – Kate Murphy

Acknowledgements

I am not on this journey without the love and support of my family. My parents worked to provide for my brother and me throughout our lives. They gave us opportunities and supported us in every way we could have imagined. My older brother served as a role model for as long as I can remember. I appreciate the time he spent playing lacrosse in the backyard with me even on the days he made me and my friends box with our lacrosse helmets and gloves! He has found tremendous success as a teacher and high school lacrosse coach, and I aspire to be the inspiration he is for his students and players.

My path to education was never planned, and I am grateful to the individuals who helped me get started and supported me along the way.

It does not happen without a visit to Chestertown, MD and Washington College. I met teammates that became life long friends and coaches who inspired me, including one assistant, Ted Greeley, who became a friend and mentor. Thank you to Ted for his service to our country in the USMC and for all he has done for me.

Thank you to Dave Taibl, fellow Washington College alum and older brother of a teammate, for thinking of me in August of 1999 as a possible solution to a last minute opening in the science department. I learned a great deal about teaching and coaching in my first four years at a boarding school.

Thank you to Tom Farquhar, Deb Donohue, and Mike Delgrande for offering me an opportunity to move up to the DMV and begin a nearly 20 year stint at Bullis School as a teacher, coach, and administrator. I appreciate the support and encouragement I received there from all of my colleagues, notably: Andy Delinsky, George Moore, Stacey Roshan, and Faith Darling. Each of them played an instrumental role in my growth and development as a school leader.

Thanks to Eric Kapitulik for helping me understand what it truly means to be a good teammate and good leader. I was introduced to Eric in 2010 and he continues to positively impact me a decade later. I am a better leader, father, husband and person because of Kap.

Thanks to former teammate, opposing coach, and competitor Andy Taibl for helping me see the bigger picture in our work with high school athletes. He helped me think about the best way to build a program and maintain consistency through hard work and commitment.

This book developed in part from conversations, reflections, and my own curiosity about how I can grow and be better. I appreciate the honest feedback and the mirror my friends hold up for me so I can more clearly see the person looking back at me. Andrew Greeley and Justin McCarthy - thank you for challenging me and reminding me of what is important in life. I am grateful to each of you.

Thank you to Darrin and Jessica Peppard as well as the entire Road to Awesome team for taking a chance on me and believing in my project. I am grateful for their commitment to me and this book.

I cannot finish without acknowledging my wife, Lauren, and our three children: Emerson, Sutton, and Hensley. Thank you, and I love you.

ABOUT THE AUTHOR

Bobby Pollicino is a career educator. He began teaching and coaching in August of 1999 and has served in a variety of roles including 15+ years as a school administrator. In addition to teaching, he also served in dean of students and assistant principal roles. Bobby has taught high school courses in science, leadership, and public speaking while also serving as a varsity assistant soccer coach and varsity head lacrosse coach. He is currently the Head of Upper School at Bullis School in Potomac, MD.

Bobby's academic leadership career is grounded in a healthy interest in leadership which has led to conferences with Stanley King Institute, Garnder Carney Leadership Institute, and a fellowship with Leadership+Design. Bobby has presented for local and national organizations on topics including meeting culture, digital wellness and hiring practices.

A native of Upstate New York, Bobby attributes many of his life lessons to observing the work ethic and commitment of his parents and older brother. He played high school and college lacrosse, winning a National Championship at the collegiate level. He has used many leadership lessons passed on from his high school and college coaches.

When not serving his school community or studying leadership, he spends time with his wife and three children. He has coached all three children in various youth sports over the years. Bobby also enjoys running and cycling as well as training in Brazilian Jiu Jitsu. He strives to be a better husband, father, leader, and person every day. A graduate of Washington College and William and Mary, Bobby lives with his family in Poolesville, MD.

MORE BOOKS FROM ROAD TO AWESOME

Taking the Leap: A Field Guide for Aspiring School Leaders
by Robert F. Breyer

Transform: Techy Notes to Make Learning Sticky
by Debbie Tannenbaum

Becoming Principal: A Leadership Journey & The Story of School Community by Dr. Jeff Prickett

Elevate Your Vibe: Action Planning with Purpose
by Lisa Toebben

#OwnYourEpic: Leadership Lessons in Owning Your Voice and Your Story by Dr. Jay Dostal

The Design Thinking, Entrepreneurial, Visionary Planning Leader: A Practical guide for Thriving in Ambiguity
by Dr. Michael Nagler

Becoming the Change: Five Essential Elements to Being Your Best Self by Dan Wolfe

inspired: moments that matter
by Melissa Wright

Foundations of Instructional Coaching: Impact People, Improve Instruction, Increase Success
by Ashley Hubner

Out of the Trenches: Stories of Resilient Educators
by Dana Goodier

Principled Leader
by Bobby Pollicino

Road to Awesome: The Journey of a Leader
by Darrin Peppard

When Calling Parents Isn't Your Calling: A teacher's guide to communicating with all parents
by Crystal Frommert

Struggle to Strength: Finding the Ingredients to Your Secret Sauce
by Kip Shubert

Guiding Transformational Change in Education
by Kristina V. Mattis

CHILDREN'S BOOKS FROM ROAD TO AWESOME

Road to Awesome A Journey for Kids
by Jillian DuBois and Darrin M. Peppard

Emersyn Blake and the Spotted Salamander
by Kim Collazo

Theodore Edward Makes a New Friend
by Alyssa Schmidt

I'm Autistic and I'm Awesome
by Derek Danziger

Emersyn Blake and the Stalked Jellyfish
by Kim Collazo

https://roadtoawesome.net/books

www.ingramcontent.com/pod-product-compliance
Lightning Source LLC
Chambersburg PA
CBHW051933160426
43198CB00012B/2133